SAATCHI & SAATCHI

THE INSIDE STORY

SAATCHI & SAATCHI
THE INSIDE STORY

ALISON FENDLEY

ARCADE PUBLISHING • NEW YORK

FIRST U.S. EDITION 1996

Library of Congress Cataloging-in-Publication Data

Fendley, Alison
    Saatchi & Saatchi : the inside story / Alison Fendley. —1st U.S. ed.
       p.   cm.
    Originally published: Commercial break, the inside story of Saatchi & Saatchi.
    ISBN 1-55970-363-6
    1. Saatchi & Saatchi—History. 2. Advertising agencies—History. I. Fendley, Alison. Commercial break, the inside story of Saatchi & Saatchi. II. Title.
HF6181.S23F45 1996
659.1'06'073—dc20   96–21077

Published in the United States by Arcade Publishing, Inc., New York
Distributed by Little, Brown and Company

10 9 8 7 6 5 4 3 2 1

BP

Designed by API

PRINTED IN THE U.S.A.

For my parents and Jeremy

What Saatchi stands for is an acronym—a priceless piece of knowledge which the gods spelled out for us in our name, letter by letter, so that we never forget it. SAATCHI—Simple And Arresting Truths Create High Impact. It's our name, it's our nature. As Martin Luther said, "Here I stand: I can do no other."

—Maurice Saatchi, July 10, 1995

CONTENTS

SAATCHI & SAATCHI
THE INSIDE STORY

one MAN WITH GLASSES LEAVES JOB

O*N DECEMBER 16, 1994*, the directors of Saatchi & Saatchi
PLC met in a boardroom on the sixth floor of the company's headquarters in the unprepossessing London neighborhood of
Fitzrovia. The subject of the meeting, which lasted for eight
hours, was supposed to be confidential, but the company was so
famous that for several days the newspapers had been rife with
speculation about its outcome. In fact, there was only one item on
the agenda: the demand by an influential group of shareholders,
led by a thirty-three-year-old Chicago fund manager named
David Herro, that Maurice Saatchi be removed from his position
as chairman (which he had held since 1985) and director of the
vast advertising network that he had founded with his brother
Charles a quarter of a century earlier.

For almost twenty-five years, his business acumen and a mesmerizing way with influential clients and Tory grandees had enabled Maurice Saatchi to forge a legendary reputation in Adland.
During that time the company had become a household name,
with its interlocking a's and puzzling origin somehow contributing to an attitude of entrepreneurial self-assurance so contagious

1

that insiders called it "the virus." For many people Saatchi & Saatchi was defined by Maurice's favorite catchphrase, "Nothing is impossible." But the man who had been known to wear outlandish scarves and Comme des Garçons suits at meetings with faceless plutocrats, City bankers, and pension-fund holders was now, it seemed, about to be ousted from his own company by a syndicate of obscure investment managers from the American Midwest. How could the most famous executive in the world of advertising have reached such a pass?

Maurice Saatchi, too, seemed to be reflecting on that question as he peered myopically out the window in his office, just down the hall from the boardroom. The view was surprisingly ordinary: it was midwinter and London had a hushed, emptied-out feeling. The weather was contributing to the city's mutedness. A spell of sleet and freezing temperatures had set in. His own face stared back at him, his flamboyantly oversized tortoiseshell spectacles reflected in the glass. He continued to wait. Now and then he went over to his white desk or paced around the dazzling white room. His step was brisk with irritation.

The current offices of Saatchi & Saatchi PLC were a significant comedown from the days before the company's financial troubles, when its headquarters occupied an imposing edifice stretching across the south end of Berkeley Square. The building's main tenant was Glaxo, the pharmaceutical giant, and yet somehow the brothers had contrived to arrange for their own name to feature prominently in big black letters on the wall above the front entrance.

Maurice Saatchi still liked to frequent the neighborhood where once Lord Lucan had played backgammon at the Clermont

Club and Prince Charles danced the night away at Annabel's, even though in the spring of 1994 the two brothers had been forced to vacate the luxurious offices on Berkeley Square. In Fitzrovia, at vast expense, Maurice and Charles had ordered a new set of offices built on the top floor, as a replica of the Berkeley Square premises. But now, in his shining tower, Maurice Saatchi was under siege.

This quality — a certain distance between image and reality — seems to have surfaced in most aspects of Maurice Saatchi's life. At forty-eight, tall and angular, with a self-deprecating air, Saatchi had often been hailed, even by his detractors, as a visionary. Yet in spite of his much-admired and enduring tactical brilliance, it could be argued that Maurice Saatchi was guilty of having cultivated the seeds of his own downfall. The campaign to evict the co-founder chairman from the board of Saatchi & Saatchi PLC had been started the previous spring by David Herro, whose Oakmark International Fund owned nearly 10 percent of Saatchi & Saatchi shares. It was Maurice's apparent indifference to costs, not to mention his lavish expenses, that had originally caused the problem. In 1994, for instance, he had claimed nearly half a million pounds in expenses. The expenses were said to include £87,000 on travel, meals, and accommodation, £33,000 on throwing a party for his wife, Josephine Hart, after the première of the film version of her novel *Damage* — it starred Jeremy Irons — and £5,600 on flowers. The blurring of Maurice Saatchi's personal affairs with company matters exasperated the firm's largest shareholders. In other respects, too, the directors who were about to fire Saatchi as chairman of the advertising company that bore his name had a formidable case. Notwithstanding his legendary client-wooing charm, Saatchi had presided over a company whose share price had plunged from £50 to 89p in 1991. It was possible that he had overreached himself, and now he was going to have to pay. Or, to use a phrase currently fashionable among the Saatchi inner circle, "Nemesis follows hubris."

In some ways David Herro and Maurice Saatchi were natural, almost archetypal opponents. Indeed anyone with a sense of Greek mythology will feel on familiar ground here. The feud between Maurice Saatchi and his stock-market Fury follows a pattern. Trial by shareholders is a ritual with its own totems, its element of mystery: unfathomable motives, contradictory evidence, missing links. And so, behind closed doors, the Saatchi board was sequestered, listening to the case against Maurice Saatchi. In the boardroom were gathered not only the members of the board themselves but also the company's financial advisers and lawyers. These professional advisers, including S. G. Warburg and the Union Bank of Switzerland, had carried out a poll of the company's biggest shareholders. Feeling was running so high, they reported, that unless the board resolved to act against Maurice Saatchi, the shareholders would call for an extraordinary general meeting and within six weeks vote him off the board themselves. The company's directors dreaded the prospect of the adverse newspaper coverage that would inevitably follow.

From time to time Maurice Saatchi was joined in his office by his brother Charles, with whom he shared a business partnership and a fraternal rivalry that reportedly reminded a former Saatchi acolyte, the public relations guru Sir Tim Bell, of Cain and Abel. In later years, Charles had become best known for his incomparable art collection and his equally incomparable temperament, but in the early days he was much celebrated for his apparent grasp of what admen call, sometimes rather pretentiously, creativity.

In the sixties and early seventies Charles Saatchi was one of the edgiest talents in what was then a small international circle of genius copywriters. He was the epitome of the adman as cultural hero: he was successful and rebellious. But something more than ambition and rebellion was fueling his erratic behavior and repeated blowups. By the late seventies, many people in the advertising business considered him a monster who shunned public gatherings and rarely condescended to see clients. Lucky Saatchi & Saatchi clients did get to meet Maurice, but most were never honored with an introduction to the enigmatic Charles. This included Margaret Thatcher, even when she was prime minister. Nevertheless his magical command of advertising voodoo was harnessed by the Conservative Party to propel Mrs. Thatcher into Downing Street and, for a decade, to polish her image from behind the scenes. Then, after years of working indefatigably for the agency, he seemed to evaporate. He disappeared — or, at any rate, he successfully transformed himself from just a very talented adman into an intriguing recluse. The man who had lifted the art of media manipulation to previously unexplored heights was himself now being called the hidden persuader.

It was true that Charles, the shy, inaccessible Saatchi brother, had never enjoyed socializing with others in the business or making long speeches at industry functions, and had never attended an annual general meeting of his own company. Yet becoming a recluse proved also to be a hugely effective ploy. It boosted his mystique, and not just because it meant that various Fleet Street newspapers had to keep reprinting photographs of Charles, the eccentric millionaire, wearing out-of-date seventies fashions.

Oddly enough, given his volatility, it is Charles and not Maurice who is remembered with the greater affection by people who have worked at Saatchi & Saatchi over the past twenty-five years. In spite of his quick temper and famously short attention span, it is hard to find anybody who has a bad word to say about him. "He has this amazing talent of making people want him to like them," says a former colleague. "People craved his approval, and they craved it even more when he withheld it, which he did only too often." Nowadays Charles Saatchi withholds more than just his approval. He has cut himself off from all but his circle of intimates, and for several years has spent less time on advertising than on his two other passions — his art collection, which is perhaps the largest private holding of contemporary painting and sculpture in the world, and go-kart racing.

In a rare public appearance two months earlier, at the award ceremony for the 1994 Turner Prize, Charles Saatchi had taken the podium at the Tate Gallery. His words were awaited with interest, for the Saatchi collection has been a focus of debate in the world of contemporary art since it opened to the public in 1985. Little is known about the inner workings of the Saatchi Gallery; even today, its finances are mysterious. And although Charles has always insisted that he is just a private collector, his collecting policy, if not his taste, is also obscure, because he has bought (and perhaps sold) so much art of so many different kinds over the last ten years. More recently, however, he has been showcasing young British artists like Damien Hirst, the object of much attention and controversy. No wonder the Tate Gallery audience looked forward with such anticipation to his prize-giving speech. In fact, what he said was typically elusive: "I'm not sure what today's young artists are putting in their porridge in the mornings," he began. "But it seems to be working. They are producing the most striking new art being made anywhere in the universe. And it seems every museum from Nebraska to Alaska is ringing up trying to organize shows of their work. And if sometimes that work is tasteless and cynical and uncouth, it's because sometimes we all are."

To a certain degree the fraternal rivalry extended into the sphere of collecting. Maurice, it is said, used to collect antique toys, but now he prefers garden bric-à-brac ("I just like a bit of old junk, a bit of column, a bit of ruin, a pergola, things like that," he says) for Old Hall, his country house in Sussex, an hour and a half's drive from London, where he and Josephine Hart give lunches attended by Tory ministers, famous playwrights, actors, publishers, and writers. It was unfortunate for Maurice that, as the board meeting in Fitzrovia dragged on, a particular document was making the rounds of Saatchi & Saatchi's head office. The January 1995 issue of *Architectural Digest* had just appeared, featuring a tour of Old Hall. "There's some sort of magic between Maurice and houses," Josephine Hart was quoted as saying, and the article went on to describe the couple's lavish renovation of the property, including the transformation of a Roman Catholic chapel, formerly used as a cloakroom, into a dining room, and the flooding of thirteen acres of pasture in order to create a lake with three islands and a boathouse.

In this atmosphere, verging on desperation, the shareholders had turned to Charles Scott, the holding company's chief executive and Maurice's chief antagonist, who rightly sensed the degree of Saatchi & Saatchi's distress. If the board retained Maurice, it ran the risk of his being forcibly removed by the shareholders; if it fired him, the subsequent fallout might damage the company beyond repair.

The rest of the building was silent. Maurice could hear nothing but the faint buzz of the air conditioning and the dull hum of traffic on Charlotte Street below. The room felt airless, the atmosphere heavy and oppressive. He moved towards the door and opened it for a quick look down the corridor. Nothing. It was as if the entire board of Saatchi & Saatchi, meeting only a few doors away to decide his future, had already packed up and gone home.

A minute later Jeremy Sinclair appeared in the room, looking shattered. Sinclair, an exceedingly soft-spoken man with a penchant for Cuban cigars, had been a Saatchi employee since the agency was founded a quarter of a century earlier, and was regarded as second only to Charles Saatchi in terms of creative talent. It was bad news, he murmured. The board had decreed that Maurice must be removed from his current position as chairman of the group. They proposed that he should instead take on the role of running Saatchi & Saatchi Advertising, the core network of advertising agencies owned by the holding company. Sinclair felt wretched: he could scarcely believe what was happening. How could the rest of the board have betrayed Maurice like this? He had spent hours trying to talk them around, but to no avail. He had been forced to accept defeat. He now slumped into a chair, exhausted.

Maurice Saatchi was (and still is) amazed by the attitude of the board members. A handful of important clients had already indicated that they would desert the company if he were removed. In fact, his ousting was the kind of event that has become increasingly common in an age of shareholder activism: in Maurice's view, the shareholders with no knowledge of the intricacies of the business had jettisoned the only person who could run the company successfully. He saw himself as the victim of a hostile takeover, as a chairman of the board who had lost out in a skirmish between the men-in-suits and the real talent.

"It was a sort of Alice in Wonderland world," Saatchi says. "Everything I considered normal and usual in the advertising business was turned upside down."

two EARLY DAYS

*T*URNING EVERYTHING UPSIDE DOWN was how the Saatchi brothers scaled the heights of the advertising world in the first place. But it was also significant that they regarded themselves as outsiders. Their background had always set them apart. It furnished them with a sort of mystery, a sort of farce: it was not uncommon in the eighties to hear Charles and Maurice Saatchi disparaged as "Italian ice-cream salesmen." In the middle of the decade Michael Wahl, the American proprietor of a large sales promotion company, was asked by a New York investment banker whether he would be interested in selling his business to Saatchi & Saatchi. "No," replied Wahl. "I don't want to sell out to the Japanese."

In fact, the Saatchi brothers were the second and third sons of an Iraqi Jewish couple. Their father was a prosperous textile merchant who imported cotton and wool products from Europe. Charles, the second son, was born in Baghdad in 1943, six years after his older brother, David. Maurice followed three years later.

The end of the Second World War brought grave political difficulties for Iraq's Jewish population. The League of Arab Nations had been formed to resist the creation of a Jewish state in

Palestine. Suddenly Jews found themselves driven out of many official jobs, a clampdown on the teaching of Hebrew was imposed, and Jewish businessmen were forced to take on Muslim partners. From the mid-forties, Nathan and Daisy Saatchi had been searching Europe for an alternative home for the family. Nathan bought two textile mills while on a visit to Britain in 1946. The following year, he sold the business in Baghdad and moved the family to Hampstead, where he had already bought a house. As it turned out, he was the forerunner of a much larger exodus — an estimated 120,000 Jews left Iraq within a few years of the Saatchi family's departure.

In Hampstead and Highgate, the Saatchi family assimilated quickly, speaking English at home even though the parents' mother tongues were Arabic and Hebrew. Some children might have recoiled from the suffocating closeness of the Saatchi home — a tall, narrow, begloomed house of small, irregular rooms overlooking the Heath. The brothers prefer not to discuss the family's life in detail, although Maurice dismisses the idea that there was anything particularly exotic about his background.

"I had a very nice, upper-middle-class upbringing in a very nice house in Hampstead," he remarks. "It was all very good and very happy, and very nice."

A different perspective is offered by Michael Green, now chairman of Carlton Communications and a childhood friend of the Saatchis, who says he has spent years arguing with the brothers about the importance of Judaism in their lives. "I am very aware of being Jewish," Green adds. "They say I am still stuck in the ghetto. They say, 'Why don't you grow up and move on? You should get out of this ghetto like we have.'"

Dissimilarities between Charles and Maurice were obvious

from the beginning. Much to the disappointment of his father, Charles never proved an academic success. Sent to Christ's College in Finchley, he failed to make a mark scholastically and took no interest in school sports or other activities either. He left at seventeen to embark on a life of wild parties and late nights. The sixties were just beginning and London was swinging.

It took Charles almost a year before he settled on advertising as the best way to express himself. During that time he worked in America, where he was exposed to the much stronger television and advertising culture. He soon discovered that he loved the advertising he saw there — it was less stuck-up than advertising in the United Kingdom and not ashamed to admit that it was out to make people buy one company's products instead of another's. Charles began to see that British ads never said what they meant. Thirty years on, he acknowledges that it was a moment of recognition; he had found his vocation. "When I started in the business I admired the stuff in the States by Doyle Dane Bernbach and other great agencies over there. It broke new ground. If I were to play a reel of best work then and put it out now, it would still look fantastic."

During the fifties and sixties, however, advertising remained an industry dominated by the old guard, by men who had grown up within the safe confines of press advertising and who had scarcely any idea of the potential of television. In Britain, the industry was not only heavily influenced by the American advertising style but also dominated by American companies. Advertising was considered an American business, and many of the biggest U.S. agencies bought up British companies in the decades after the war, while retaining their headquarters in New York, still considered very much the industry's heart. These U.S. outsiders brought with them new techniques, and the British found themselves exposed for the first time to a much wider range of marketing services — public relations and more sophisticated research methods, for example. Large British corporations were quick to discover that American companies had more to offer than their British rivals. Chief among these American agencies in sixties London was J. Walter Thompson, with its reputation for gentlemanlike business practices. This was a time when the advertising industry's trade body, the Institute of Practitioners in Advertising, banned companies from soliciting the clients of their rivals.

Charles Saatchi's first visit to America was a timely one. American advertising had been reinvented in the early sixties by Bill Bernbach's Volkswagen ads, which prompted buyers to fall in love with the ugly but reliable Beetle. The blend of humor and hard sell signaled a major change. The other mover and shaker in American advertising at the time was the British-born David Ogilvy, whose own brand of jargon and pseudoscience highlighted the industry's craving for respectability. The adman's wish to be treated as a member of the professional classes was nurtured by Ogilvy in his once influential but now perhaps somewhat outdated guide to the industry, *Confessions of an Advertising Man*. First published in 1963, the book was immediately adopted by the industry's leading players, who devoured its various chapters on "How to manage an advertising agency," "How to write potent copy," and "How to make good television commercials." In other words, it was immediately seized upon as a rule book that showed that advertising, like science, follows certain principles.

While David Ogilvy was drawing up his formula for successful advertising, new types of research were gaining in popularity. People were becoming more sophisticated consumers in the sixties, more confident about spending money. Unfortunately, this also meant they were becoming less easy to predict, so advertising agencies started calling on academics with their flow charts, performance models, tables of evaluation, and fancy formulas for help. Claiming to show once and for all that advertising really does work, that it actually results in the sale of more boxes of laundry detergent or cans of baked beans, this research brought with it a whole new language, a series of pseudotechnical terms impossible for the uninitiated to decipher, which gave the advertising industry, or so it hoped, a more professional, more scientific image.

In the same way, admen began to group members of the public by social class, giving each a different letter: A, B, or C at the more affluent and better-educated end, and D and E at the bottom of the ladder. Snappy jargon became popular. AIDA, for example, was introduced as shorthand for the idea that an advertisement must capture Attention, arouse Interest, and make potential consumers Desire a product so much that they will rush out and take Action to buy it. VIPS was another acronym, meaning an ad has to be Visible, to Identify the product, to Promise to do this with some benefit, and to do it with Simplicity.

The money spent on this kind of scientific research and terminology was probably more a reflection of the industry's own insecurities than of anything else. At the turn of the century the first Lord Leverhulme, Britain's original margarine and soap king, made the celebrated remark that half of the money he spent on advertising was wasted, but he wasn't sure which half. The value of a scientific approach was given most credibility in postwar America, as more and more advertising agencies recruited psychologists. One of the forefathers of modern advertising research, Ernest Dichter, developed a controversial new way of trying to understand why people chose one brand of laundry detergent rather than another and why they were happy to buy some products while refusing to buy others. Working in the fifties, Dichter pioneered a technique called motivational research, which attempted to fathom the subconscious factors that influence people's behavior. The theory depended on finding "triggers" or reflexes that would lead to large numbers of people behaving in a predetermined way. It was all about locating people's vulnerabilities — such as their need to conform or their need for security — and then using them to help to sell virtually anything.

Inevitably there was a backlash. Vance Packard, in his 1953 book *The Hidden Persuaders,* outlined his conspiracy theory alleging that shoppers were constantly being duped by advertising campaigns that set out primarily to work upon their feelings and half-conscious attitudes by nonrational suggestion. And yet the distinction between the "informational advertising" prescribed by Ogilvy and the "advertising by psychological manipulation" identified by Packard was always a rough-and-ready one. "Pavement contracting: driveways and paths resurfaced from 50¢ a square yard: phone ———" falls clearly enough in the one category, while "It's smart to drink Port" belongs unmistakably to the other. But it might be rather more problematic to reach agreement on a classification for the single-line advertisement that appeared in the *New Statesman's* personal column for many years: "French-taught Parisienne; Results guaranteed." In early 1995 John Philip Jones, a professor of communications at Syracuse University, published the findings of his new survey, which concluded that on average just half of all advertising actually does work, thus suggesting that the pseudoscience of advertising has not made a lot of progress in the century after Lord Leverhulme.

Despite the books, the acronyms, the experiments, and a growing body of memoirs and reminiscences, the history of advertising is full of gaps and uncertainty. The sixties are particularly hazy. In the helter-skelter of the time, there were lots of casualties. Advertising was often disorderly and chaotic, as Charles soon discovered. At first he joined a small agency, but he quickly left. "It was a very bad agency and he thought what they were doing was garbage," said a colleague from his early days. After a short time without a job, he went to study design at a local college until he got his first break in the advertising world, at the age of twenty-two. In 1965 Jack Stanley, the creative director of Benton & Bowles, a large American-owned agency based in Knightsbridge, hired Charles Saatchi as a junior copywriter. He was assigned to work with a twenty-one-year-old art director, John Hegarty, who has since gone on to run his own agency, Bartle Bogle Hegarty.

Hegarty had joined the firm that year as an assistant art director straight out of college. He recalls, "I was hired as a Young Turk, and after a week or so Jack Stanley wandered into my office and said, 'I've found a young copywriter to work with you.' I said, 'What's his name?' Jack replied, 'Charles Saatchi,' and I said to myself, 'Oh, shit — Italian, probably lives at home with his mum and can't spell — just my luck.' I was right on two counts, but he wasn't Italian."

Right away, Charles Saatchi did attention-getting, formula-smashing work. The ads that resulted were brilliant — cheeky, witty, knowing. "Charlie Saatchi was one of the inventors of modern British advertising, because he brought comparative advertising to Britain," says Robin Wight, the chairman of London's WCRS agency. "British advertising had always had a whimsical streak, because the traditional person in British advertising was a failed poet or novelist. But British people don't like selling. And Charlie Saatchi took the straightness and candor of the American approach and Britishized it — added wit, added an art-directed style, added irony. You know, an American with irony is an Englishman."

He landed his first assignments at a propitious moment. Soon Charles teamed up with the senior art director at the agency, Ross Cramer. They later moved together to Collett Dickinson Pearce, one of London's most creative agencies at the time. Colin Millward was in charge at CDP in those days and was someone Charles greatly admired, but CDP was important to Charles for another reason. It was there that he met an account handler called David Puttnam and a "creative" by the name of Alan Parker. Puttnam remembers Charles in the early days as somebody who was single-minded, not manically ambitious, but extremely idiosyncratic, and focused on things that interested him. "There was no middle ground — you either captured his interest or you didn't," he says. "He had a way of generating excitement. He had this strange walk, very fast, with his head down and his shoulders forward. Still has it. He always had this fantastic lateral mind," Puttnam adds. "His ideas would come in from left field. For Selfridges, we used to wander around the store on a Monday morning, we'd have lunch at the store, and then we'd decide which department we'd go see. And we'd spend the afternoon. Then we had to have the ad done by Tuesday morning. Charlie saw retail as show business. He really got off on that campaign."

Puttnam, in turn, encouraged Charles to think about writing for film. Cramer and Saatchi had various ideas and Puttnam got Parker to write one of them up into a screenplay. Hegarty recalls that the film eventually got made as *Sealed with a Loving Kiss* (called *Melody* in the U.S.). "It was about a couple of young twelve-year-olds who fall in love and run away. It came from a story in a newspaper, and it sank without trace. Mind you, we were always told it was big in Japan — that was the great phrase that we had."

Charles apparently had several other ideas for movies, but his advertising work took off so quickly that he was unable to develop any of them. Puttnam is convinced that he had the potential and originality of thought to be a success in the film industry. "He has a very good sense of the audience, and a low boredom threshold, which the audience also tends to have," he says. "I think he would have been far more successful than I am."

Part of the reason for Charles Saatchi's success in advertising was his contempt for the rules. He experienced his first taste of controversy at an early age, while still working with Ross Cramer at Collett Dickinson Pearce. Together they had written a campaign for Ford, producing a series of ads that compared the company's cars to competitors such as Jaguars and Rovers. One of Charles's ads showed a new Cortina overtaking an older car under the slogan "They appear the same — but disappear differently." A subsequent ad claimed, "The Ford Executive compares quite favorably with these grand cars," next to a table of statistics revealing that Ford outperformed Jaguar, Rover, and Mercedes in many categories. It is difficult today to imagine the kind of outrage such an advertisement caused. At the time, however, those ads breached IPA rules, although the guidelines were later changed to allow what is now commonly referred to as "knocking copy."

Very soon the industry began to recognize the quality of his copywriting. Edward Booth-Clibborn, chairman of the Designers & Art Directors Association (D & AD), set up in 1962 to encourage high standards in visual communication, remembers Charles as one of the most assiduous of the young admen in trying to get his work accepted by the jury that each year selected the best advertising work. In 1967 the Selfridges ad, written at CDP, was included, the following year the Ford ad.

"He was very exceptional," Booth-Clibborn says. "This was very much the period of what I call the breakthrough of creative work in this country. Up to that time we were copying American slang, and now for the first time we started to use our own language in advertising. And these people, particularly Alan Parker and Charles Saatchi, started using colloquial English that gave a special identity to their work. Charles Saatchi was very conscious of doing work that got visibility, particularly through the D & AD awards, but he and some of the others at the time really believed in D & AD and what we stood for. They were still an isolated group in the industry, but they believed in improving creative standards; that was the important thing."

Only a year after changing jobs, Charles and Ross Cramer were on the move again, this time to a smaller firm. But it was a disaster and after just six months they decided to go it alone, launching a consultancy that would write ads on a freelance basis for well-established agencies. Cramer Saatchi opened its doors from small offices on Goodge Street, above a fast-food restaurant. In the same building David Puttnam was beginning to make films.

Cramer and Saatchi put much emphasis on the idea of focus. "I learned the art of focusing on one thing from Charles Saatchi a long time ago," says John Hegarty, who soon joined the consultancy. "Charlie would just look at something and say, this is the problem, that's what we need to solve. He just concentrated on that until it was solved. There was no periphery involved, nothing distracted him. And what was great is that he didn't mind where the idea came from. All that mattered was that it was a good idea."

Cramer Saatchi was introduced to its most important client, the Health Education Council, almost by accident. Ross Cramer had a child at the same school as a woman who worked there and, as they waited to collect their children one day, she happened to mention that her boss was looking for an advertising agency. At first the work consisted of producing brochures and posters, but later the HEC invested in full-scale advertising. Charles Saatchi created a number of antismoking ads, including one carrying a picture of a disgusting-looking black substance with the copyline "The tar and discharge that collects in the lungs of an average smoker." Another showed a hand being scrubbed with a nailbrush and the caption "You can't scrub your lungs clean."

The HEC campaign served to draw media attention to Cramer Saatchi for the first time. The *Sun* wrote a story about the antismoking campaign, noting how dynamic and brutally effective the copywriting had seemed in comparison with the rather uninspired work being put out by the rest of the London advertising world. Charles Saatchi saw his opportunity. He realized that in the future he would have to devote much of his energy to getting the press interested in his advertisements while remaining out of the limelight himself. This was a departure from the traditional way advertising agencies got themselves noticed, by virtue of the charismatic personalities running them — people like David Ogilvy, who shamelessly pushed himself into the public spotlight.

Charles proved a consummate public relations man. He understood instictively how useful the press could be to his business. He courted journalists from the advertising industry's most prominent trade magazine, *Campaign*. He passed them news and industry gossip before it was common knowledge and in return received generous coverage for his agency. Journalists said he had a knack of making even the most boring stories sound interesting. He carried on a very effective one-man publicity drive over the telephone.

It was Jeremy Sinclair who devised another ad for the Health Education Council, the one that remains the company's benchmark: a glum-looking man in a V-neck sweater clutching his swollen belly above the words "Would you be more careful if it was you that got pregnant?" The aim was simple: to get more men to think about contraception. John Hegarty, who also worked on the account, remembers the first time he saw the design for what turned out to be one of the most famous ads of the past twenty-five years: "Charlie rushed out with a layout to show me. It was the pregnant man. I almost died. It was the best thing I had ever seen. Its simplicity and audacity were electrifying. I had been writing lines like 'Who taught your daughter the facts of life?' with a picture of a pregnant gym-slipped girl. The pregnant man was more than just a piece of advertising; it was the first time that I had seen a piece of work that moved beyond the accepted boundaries our business operated in, commanding attention from a far wider group of people."

When Saatchi & Saatchi was formed several months later, the pregnant man was used to launch the creative reputation of the new agency. Charles recognized its potential as a media story, and articles about it ran in the press for weeks. Likewise, all the various Saatchi campaigns would convey some essential qualities of the sixties: the sexual freedom, the growing gulf between men and women. Without clichés, Charles Saatchi put these elements into advertising.

The balance of power between the intuitive Charles and the more analytic Maurice was from the beginning unequal. Maurice was quieter and shyer than his raucous brother; he was also more studious, graduating with a degree from the London School of Economics. His tutors felt that he was talented and hard-working enough to enter academic life, but Maurice Saatchi had other ideas. He had his eyes fixed on the world of business. He joined Haymarket Publishing, a small but fast-growing company controlled at the time by Michael Heseltine, the Tory MP, and Lindsay Masters. Among its range of periodicals was *World Press News,* a struggling title for people who worked in journalism or advertising. Maurice was recruited to help relaunch this rather plain magazine, which turned into one of the most successful trade publications in the country, *Campaign.* It was an immediate success, with news and gossip about the advertising industry on the front page and features and comment pieces inside. It was brash, even sensationalist, compared to usual trade papers, but it was quickly adopted by the advertising fraternity. At twenty-four, Maurice was driving to his office every day in a flashy 1966 Corvette, while many young men of his generation would have been glad to possess an old rattletrap.

Charles too, now a leading copywriter notable for his wild hairstyle and beatnik clothes, was able to indulge an obsession with cars. "He seemed to have a new car every second week," David Puttnam recalls, "each one more glamorous and more unusual and noisier than before."

Meanwhile Charles was watching his brother's early success. He was impressed with Maurice's business acumen and his conscientious attitude to hard work. By 1970 Charles was itching for his own advertising agency, but his partner Ross Cramer had no desire to get involved in the launch of just another small London agency. So when Cramer opted for a career as a director of television commercials, Charles decided Maurice would make the perfect business partner. "I think Maurice was rather surprised at first," says a former colleague who knows both brothers well. "For years, Maurice was always in the shadow of Charles. Even if he wasn't really, he felt as if he was."

Advertising agencies rarely follow their own marketing advice when it comes to picking a name. They tell their clients to choose something short, snappy, and memorable for their new products, while burdening their own companies with some of the longest and most complicated strings of surnames imaginable. There can be few other businesses in which absurd names like Still Price Court Twivy D'Souza, for example, are fairly typical. Charles's new agency was originally to be called Saatchi Cramer and Saatchi. But with the disappearance of his other partner, this was refined to Saatchi & Saatchi. Perhaps he recognized that the reduplicated exotic name — with the ampersand in the middle like a magic charm — possessed a kind of mysterious allure: "half sturdy Saab, half decadent Häagen-Dazs," according to the *New Yorker.* "It's a bloody good name for a new advertising agency," Charles told his brother. "Saatchi & Saatchi — it's so bizarre no one will forget it in a hurry."

"I remember him making a joke of the name," recalls Chris Martin, then a junior copywriter at the consultancy. "He said they had to have a name that people would remember, so he had got his brother in to make sure they had the right name, almost as if that was the only reason he was joining."

Maurice spent months carefully planning the new agency. His task was to organize the finances, and over the summer of 1970 he approached Lindsay Masters, his boss at Haymarket, for £25,000 in capital. Masters, who came in as a private investor, kept his links with Saatchi & Saatchi secret, as he knew that his position as the head of the company that owned *Campaign* could be an embarrassment. But rumors of a clandestine link between the new agency and the industry's influential trade paper were quick to ignite among the many admen jealous of Saatchi & Saatchi's frequent and favorable press coverage. Masters's Haymarket partner, Michael Heseltine, was also approached, although by that time he had become a minister in the Heath government and was forced to decline the offer. Other backers included fashion designer Mary Quant and her husband, Alexander Plunket-Greene. Two years later, when the Saatchis bought her out, Quant made nearly four times her investment in profit. "I don't remember the figures," she says. "I just had lunch with Maurice and realized he was brilliant."

With the financing in place, Maurice was able to put the final touches on his five-year plan for the agency, which included a share structure for a possible public flotation. The advertising industry of the time, with its high costs and small capital assets, was not held in very high esteem by the City, London's financial community. In 1966 David Ogilvy was the first to take his agency public, in London and New York simultaneously. In Britain, up to the early seventies, only two agencies had gone public: Dorland Advertising, which had got itself into trouble when it was bought in 1971 by an opportunistic arbitrageur, John Bentley, who then stripped it of its property assets; and S. H. Benson, which was bought by Jacob Rothschild and then sold on to Ogilvy & Mather. Nevertheless, Maurice insisted that a flotation was an essential part of the five-year plan. After all, the Saatchi brothers wanted to build a big advertising agency and a creative one — impossible, according to received wisdom in the industry, which said agencies could be either small and good or big and boring.

In September 1970, Saatchi & Saatchi started life as it meant to go on — in the headlines. Using his close relationship with journalists on *Campaign*, Charles Saatchi planned the media offensive he hoped would put the agency on the map. For years he had invested energy feeding news and gossip over the telephone to eager journalists; now it was their turn. On the morning of Friday, September 11, the headline "Saatchi starts agency with £1 million" was splashed across the front page of *Campaign*, alongside a picture of Charles and Maurice. Coverage continued inside with a full-page feature on the new agency and its rosy prospects under the two brothers, "each caught up in the infectious enthusiasm of the other."

The story had all the hallmarks of Saatchi bluster: not even the most creative accountant could have made the value of the new agency's accounts add up to anything like £1 million (the true figure was probably a quarter of that amount). This was partly industry convention, but it was also characteristic of the Saatchi style — promise anything now and then work out how it could be achieved later. "The agency is strongly orientated towards the creative side and much interest will now centre on whether it can be as successful as the Cramer Saatchi consultancy, which is now folding," said the *Campaign* story. "For while admiring the work of Saatchi and art director Ross Cramer, critics have claimed that it is one thing to run a consultancy doing new presentations in a marketing vacuum and another to run advertising that must run in the open market."

In addition to the *Campaign* story, Charles decided to buy publicity in the form of a full-page advertisement in the *Sunday*

Times. The ad was heavy on copy and ran under the title "Why I think it's time for a new kind of advertising." Signed by Jeremy Sinclair, the piece was actually written by Haymarket director and *Observer* journalist Robert Heller. It attacked old-fashioned agency structures, particularly the account men, or suits, whose job it was to form a link between the client and the creatives, the people in the agency who write the ads.

The brothers deliberately cast themselves in the role of outsiders taking on the establishment. They were, self-consciously, upstarts — but they were upstarts with big ideas. "From the day the advertising agency started," Maurice says, "when we had only eleven people, we always tried to look grander than we were." In the opinion of Cecil Parkinson, former chairman of the Conservative Party, the secret of the brothers' early success was their ability to turn disadvantage to advantage and the way they exploited their position as outsiders. "They were not stereotypes in any way," he says. "Charles is just a brilliant copywriter, this evasive character who really prefers to have only a limited contact with the world. And never in a million years would you think Maurice was English, because he has this interesting approach to things. He has a style of his own. He has tuned in very well to Britain, and knows how the system works, but he also has a very individualistic attitude, and I think some of that stems from his unusual background."

three SWINGING SEVENTIES

*T*HE SWINGING SIXTIES came to advertising a decade late. The seventies were a time of experimentation, of pushing back accepted boundaries, and this pioneering spirit was deliberately exploited by Saatchi & Saatchi. From the outset, the brothers made it clear that they intended to promote the advertising agency just as much as the products featured in their ads. Having embraced this important principle, Charles and Maurice Saatchi were not inhibited, even for a moment, by the fact they had just two clients, a handful of staff, and two modest floors of office space. "I thought they had more ambition than anyone else," recalls Michael Bungey, now chairman of Bates Worldwide. "They were terrific lateral thinkers. They were more daring. Quite simply, they had more balls than anyone else."

By coincidence, the seventies also provided a favorable setting for Charles's single-minded vision of advertising. At the time most copywriting ranged from the trite ("Why don't we do this more often?") through the vulgarly inane ("I'm Debbie. Fly me to the moon over Miami") to the idiotically bizarre ("I dreamed I stopped traffic in my Maidenform bra"). Charles broke the industry's rules by running campaigns that were often shocking and radical, and his slogans always went to the heart of the matter. "The Saatchis timed their arrival perfectly — or rather their parents did," wrote Jeremy Bullmore, chairman of J. Walter Thompson in London, in the *Guardian* in October 1987. "Before the Saatchi phenomenon, those of us in this surprisingly small industry (only 15,000 people in the whole of this country) were accustomed to obscurity. No agency was a household name, very few people knew what agencies did, the City of London had never met us and didn't want to, and the feeling was mutual. More importantly, we'd all been brought up to believe that the function of agencies was to make brands and clients famous and profitable while remaining decently anonymous ourselves."

Yet there was another, perhaps more important, difference between Saatchi & Saatchi and its competitors. The new company was not only dynamic, its nine staff members were all relatively young. Paul Bainsfair, who was recruited by Maurice and Charles, observes that in the early days the agency's most striking feature was its personnel, not its product. "I knew they had done some good work," he says, "but actually you were aware of the agency because they were the new kids on the block. When I got to Saatchi I couldn't believe what a meritocracy it was. You had twenty-seven-year-olds walking around as directors."

Charles Saatchi had never been involved in the management of an advertising agency; he had never come into direct contact with clients before. Nevertheless, he realized that it was necessary for the company to find a more prestigious location. While the modest Goodge Street garret had served Cramer Saatchi well, the new agency needed to be in a place that would impress clients, a place with a boardroom and plenty of space to expand. Maurice went out on a search and found suitable premises in Soho. The new agency took the ground floor and basement of a rather elegant building on Golden Square.

At first Charles had believed that he could dispense with old-fashioned account executives. Soon, however, he began to realize that a good media man would be crucial to the success of an agency that had promised to buy advertising cheaper than anybody else. The Saatchi brothers had been told that Paul Green was currently the best in the field. Unfortunately, Green had ideas about starting a business of his own. Second on the brothers' list was a man called Tim Bell, then media director at Geers Gross. Bell recalls, "In 1970 Charles Saatchi rang me up and said, 'I hear you're the best media man in Britain, why don't you join us?' He was starting an agency — there were to be only nine of us, we only had two accounts and he was only twenty-six (I was twenty-eight and Maurice was twenty-four). It was a massive leap in the dark, but he had done the pregnant-man ad and I thought that was the best ad I had ever seen, so I said yes."

Others quickly came on board, including Ron Collins, a twenty-nine-year-old art director who later went on to found the agency Wight Collins Rutherford Scott. Alan Tilby joined from Charles's former agency Collett Dickinson Pearce, while John Hegarty, Jeremy Sinclair, Bill Atherton, and Chris Martin stayed on from the Cramer Saatchi consultancy. Hegarty remembers that when the agency was first launched, Charles made a great effort to become a businessman, cutting his hair and even wearing a suit every day to the office. "When he started the agency, he suddenly became a banker," he goes on. "Even the Saatchi & Saatchi letterhead was designed to look like a bank. I suppose Charles wanted to establish a creative reputation — though people were still frightened by it, and thought people at the new agency were all mad, and worried that people would go berserk and crazy at any moment. So what Charles did was to present himself very conventionally. I guess he was saying, 'Look, I'm just throwing you slightly,' because people thought, 'Hey, wait a minute, if you're so creative, why are you dressed like this?' In other words, he was always setting up a conflict to keep them off balance, and him on the front foot."

In the *Sunday Times* advertisement Saatchi & Saatchi promised to replace this account man with "a coordinator who is not briefed by the client, does not brief the creative people, does not pass judgment on ads and does not present ads to the client, but works with the creators as a day-to-day administrator." In reality there were no coordinators. Another Saatchi illusion.

There is a photograph of Tim Bell with Charles and Maurice, taken in 1970 at the time of the agency's launch, in which a classically profiled Charles looks demurely downward; a boyish Maurice, in half-profile, gazes pensively, perhaps a little strangely, into the middle distance; and Tim Bell, wearing a wide-cut seventies style tie, stares straight into the camera, his features set in an expression of almost harsh resolve. Without Bell's determination — and by the end of the agency's first year he was already making good his ambition to move out of media buying, the job of negotiating the best price for advertising time on television or in the press, into a more central role — it is doubtful whether the phenomenal rise and rise of Saatchi & Saatchi would have taken place.

Despite his boast in the *Sunday Times* that the agency would not be employing account men, it took Charles only a matter of months to realize they needed someone to help Tim Bell and Maurice drum up new business. A young Australian-born adman named Bill Muirhead was recruited in 1972 and soon became the prototype for such appointments, according to Jeremy Sinclair. "Charles had read in a book somewhere that tall people do better in business, so all account men had to be tall — six foot tall. You see, that was the sort of snippet he used to pick up and think, yes, that's a good idea, we'll have tall account men, people have confidence in tall people. Because we started off without any account men at all, so Bill was the first model. He was tall — this was the rule for account men." Media men and creatives, on the other hand, could be any height they liked. "That was just a Charlie joke," recalls Tim Bell. "If account men were tall and elegant with nice voices and good manners, they got on better with clients than ones who were short, fat, and ugly and swore. I suppose that tells you something about working in a service industry."

Almost from the beginning of Tim Bell's years with the agency, *Campaign* started calling him the third Saatchi brother. Indeed, he often used to refer to himself as the ampersand in Saatchi & Saatchi. Muirhead is in no doubt about the contribution Bell made to the company in those early days. "He was probably one of the greatest salesmen of anything that I ever met. He had charisma, energy, the lot. Me and other account handlers were totally in awe of him. He was mesmerizing. You thought, I could never be as good as that no matter how hard I tried." According to Paul Bainsfair, the brothers created the agency's atmosphere and perhaps had a vision of how they wanted the company to develop, but they were reluctant to have any interface with clients. "Tim was the man who made it happen. He was a fantastic adman, the best presenter in town, with a natural gift of making all clients fall in love with him the minute they met him. If you ask me, Tim Bell was probably the single most important reason why the agency was a success."

Nowadays, however, Bell says the stories about him as the third brother are completely untrue. "I was a third partner and had equity in the company and we carved up all the jobs between us," he says. "There were three offices at Saatchi & Saatchi in those days, Charlie's, Maurice's, and mine; the rest was open plan. In some ways, the brothers did operate on a divide-and-rule basis, using all sorts of management techniques to keep control of people and divide them against each other."

Still, for Charles Saatchi advertising was primarily about the ads and their slogans, not all the mind games and support services that had grown up around them in the preceding decades. Making things — visual and verbal — was his dominating passion. It was also, in a paradoxical way, his link to the Ogilvy past that he was at such pains to repudiate. As far as he was concerned, Ogilvy's approach, with its pseudoscientific research, was a waste of money. His *Sunday Times* manifesto had tried to steal the high ground by deploring old-fashioned, unimaginative advertising that never got noticed, even if it was supported by reams of careful research. "A creative ad is only an exercise in self-indulgence unless it achieves the client's marketing purposes, expressed in concrete terms of sales penetration," it said, "and a marketing agency cannot achieve any result, except in the expensive duplication of its clients' own marketing and merchandising skills, unless it creates ads that seize the public mind."

In practice, the commitment to original copywriting and art direction involved a lot of extra work by agency staff. Paul Bainsfair says it was not unusual to find people staying in the office and working overnight. "Saatchi's was an amazing place in those days, and over time you got into the swing of the thing and thought you were invincible — like a mass psychosis. People changed. You became convinced that you were bigger and stronger and tougher. It was like a cult Moonie thing. I used to feel sorry for other agencies when we were pitching, because I was convinced there was no way they could beat the kind of effort we put in."

Charles Saatchi brought the Health Education Council account with him from Cramer Saatchi. He quickly realized that the agency could extend its controversial campaign to television in a way that would grab the attention of a national audience. The first color TV commercial was broadcast in Britain in 1969. Most TV ads were for soaps and detergents and were boring and unimaginative in their approach to selling. They were tired, patronizing, and irritating, but relatively effective if repeated enough times. Though the first television commercial had been broadcast in 1955, advertising agencies were still struggling to adapt to a medium that would soon change the industry beyond all recognition. Many early TV ads suffered from being only black and white, while others were little more than elaborate newspaper campaigns roughly adapted for television. Of course, there were some early exceptions. The Gold Box Benson & Hedges cigarette ads, created by Collett Dickinson Pearce, stood out from a very average crowd, for example, with their use of actors such as Dudley Moore. But there was still no automobile advertising on TV, and commercial breaks were dominated in the main by ultraconventional ads for indistinguishable food items and packaged goods.

One of Saatchi & Saatchi's first HEC television ads depicted smokers crossing Waterloo Bridge, intercut with a film of lemmings throwing themselves recklessly off the edge of a cliff. The voice-over said: "There's a strange Arctic rodent called a lemming which every year throws itself off a cliff. It's as though it wanted to die. Every year in Britain thousands of men and women smoke cigarettes. It's as though they want to die. . . ."

Other ads in the campaign helped to consolidate Saatchi's reputation. For example, another featured a quizmaster promising, "If you smoke forty cigarettes a day you, yes, you, could win a case of chronic bronchitis." Meanwhile Jeremy Sinclair wrote a series of ads about people who had managed to give up smoking by hypnosis or eating prunes or chewing gum. On the other hand, women were targeted by an uncompromising ad that showed a newborn baby in an incubator with the line "Poor thing. It's so weak because the mother smoked during pregnancy."

It was important for the new agency to recruit new clients. The Citrus Marketing Board of Israel, which sold its fruit under the Jaffa brand name, was thinking about funding an advertising campaign to help it cash in on the boycott of South African oranges. The young Saatchi & Saatchi saw its opportunity, prepared a pitch, and won the account. Unfortunately, its best advertising line never appeared. "Jaffa: the Chosen Fruit" was banned by the television advertising watchdogs on the grounds that it was anti-Semitic — in spite of the fact that the agency responsible for the ad was run by Jews who insisted that it was not offensive.

"Charles saw everything as a kind of billboard," says Bill Muirhead. "The shortest number of words, the most powerful, simple expression of the message. He would be sitting there at his desk, and his mind would be going, and then, in his little hand-writing, he would write it. And in one case he wrote the copy on an actual orange and photographed it — this in a campaign for Jaffa oranges — and he said, 'That's it. There's the ad. Go and do it.' And we set the copy up on an actual orange and photographed it. Simple as that. I kept some of the drawings, because I thought some day it might be worth something."

For a time, Saatchi & Saatchi knew nothing but success. "I've never seen an agency function so effectively," says Martin Sorrell, the former Saatchi group finance director who is now head of WPP, the largest advertising company in the world. "This brilliant flair for publicity, brilliant control — some would call it manipulation — of publicity. Every week, there would be another headline: 'Saatchi wins another million-pound campaign.' And Maurice was one of the first to think strategically about the business instead of just tactically. There was an IPA convention that you didn't go and pitch the clients of other members of the IPA, but since the Saatchis weren't members of the IPA, they pitched those clients and often got them. It was really what Maurice used to call the art of the impossible. We were in the coup business."

The headlines in *Campaign* and elsewhere ensured that Charles's reputation as the elusive and mercurial genius behind the scenes grew apace. He understood the value of publicity, but his style had its cost. Over the years there were nightmarish scenes marked by tantrums, feuds, and other lavish displays of temperament. "In those days Charles was like a consummate dictator," says a former colleague. "He was the god that we all did it for; he was incredibly powerful and charismatic." After one new business pitch Muirhead went to Charles, "and I said how brilliant I thought Tim was, he is a complete genius, and Charles completely put him down — he's a little worm, he dragged him up from the gutter — all done with a smile on his face."

In the early days Charles was writing many of the ads himself. He was notoriously uncompromising, refusing to allow a client to reject his work — or even accept it — until Charles was completely satisfied with it himself. He was interested only in ads he thought would make a difference, and he had little time for some of the precious egos of the people who worked for him. Bell remembers an occasion when he had taken one of Ron Collins's ads to a client who had wanted some changes made to it. During the meeting Bell had written the corrections on the ads themselves. When he got back to the office Collins exploded with anger. "Who the hell do you think you are, writing on my ads?" screamed Collins. Charles in turn exploded, and screamed at Collins, "Who the fuck do you think *you* are? Michel-fucking-angelo?"

"Charles has got a very violent temper," a Saatchi director says. "In the old days, he would beat Maurice up, physically, in the office. One day he said to Maurice, 'I can't believe you came out of the same womb that I did,' and then picked up a chair and ran down the table and hit Maurice on the head with it. What it would usually be about was that Charles had spent a lot of time trying to get the ad right, but there Maurice would be, rehearsing the presentation and looking slightly bored. So Charles would be — boom!"

Jeremy Sinclair said that Charles created waves and there were some people in the agency who were great on surfboards. Rather enigmatic, unassuming and private, Sinclair used to have lunch with Charles every day in order to discuss work. Otherwise he tended to keep to himself. He seemed happy to remain in Charles's shadow, his only diversion being a regular attendance at meetings of a charity by the name of the School of Economic Science. Tim Bell thinks the school gave Sinclair a sense of equilibrium; perhaps it kept him well enough balanced that he never got affected by the blowups at the agency. "He didn't talk to us about the organization. We always used to call it his red fire engine, because they have this sort of mantra they say over and over again, and we always imagined Jeremy sitting in the corner saying, 'Red fire engine, red fire engine,' until he calmed down."

Not everybody adapted to Charles's violent moods with such equanimity. Paul Bainsfair observes that he was an incredibly powerful personality, in the sense that he had an explosive temper. However, the resident genius would never shout at or be angry with anybody not at the top of the company. "Even so, you'd hear these stories coming back about how he got mad and belted someone or beat up Maurice in a meeting or held Martin Sorrell up by his lapels in the boardroom, and somehow it increased his stature in your eyes — so we were all in awe of him."

On occasion, Charles would deal with clients himself. He could be utterly charming when he wanted to be, but he soon decided to bow out of making the presentations. "I think he stopped because a couple of times he got to the point where he nearly came to blows with the client," Bill Muirhead says. To those who worked at the agency, however, his tantrums were as violent as ever. He stormed around the office, demanding better ideas and harder work, while having the kind of tempestuous relationship with Maurice that only brothers could survive. Even while Maurice was busy making hundreds of cold calls to potential clients, drumming up new business in a way that broke the long-established rules of an industry that banned such opportunistic behavior, he fought with his brother. Their rows were legendary at Golden Square.

Some of the craziness and drama was funny. Muirhead recounts stories about Charles throwing chairs at Maurice in his rages, screaming and punching. "It was usually about pitches, because everything gets tense then." In particular, he remembers rehearsing an important pitch for Hygena Kitchens. "Charles decided he was too nervous to present the ads, as it was a big account, and so Maurice was presenting ads. The trouble is, Maurice finds it difficult to rehearse properly, so he was being rather offhand. You know, 'Here's for an ad for furniture, and here's an ad for wall units' — that sort of thing. He wasn't taking the piss, but it was a bit like that, and then suddenly I heard this scream of rage as Charles just exploded. 'Hey, you're not taking this seriously!' Next thing he ran around the table after Maurice — we had rush matting on the floor — and Maurice ran the other way and tripped, and Charles picked up a light aluminum chair and hit him. It was a frightening sight. Maurice was scared, and Tim tried to stop it but inadvertently got in the way, so he was hit as well."

Usually these rows came and went pretty quickly and Maurice seemed able to shrug them off. But Tim Bell, a very personable young man who wanted to maintain a convivial working atmosphere if possible, took them more to heart. When he found the battles too much, he would try to intervene, only to find both Charles and Maurice turning their fury on him.

In the early days Tim Bell, Bill Muirhead, and Ron Leagas, a new recruit, did most of the account handling, but Charles kept abreast of each project. He wouldn't take part in the pitch himself, but soon afterwards he would ring up the client, pretending to be from *Campaign*. According to Ron Leagas, he was elusive because he was shy. "I think he was nervous in the early days, because here was a young agency and he'd never had to deal with clients before. And then, I suppose, the more the agency grew in the absence of any client contact with him, the more he felt justified and obliged to stay distant. As a matter of fact, I quite often got Charles to come into pitches, but most of the time he'd say, 'Don't be daft, I'll fuck it up,' and, yes, he might have done, because not everyone is able to handle that stark simplicity. So I think he painted himself into a corner."

Joining at the impressionable age of twenty-four, Bill Muirhead loved the fact that everyone at the agency was young and energetic. "I was given this incredible freedom to do things without any rules, no one saying this is the way it's got to be done. I was brought up in the traditional agency where rules and regulations did not encourage creative thought. It was as though David Ogilvy had done it all and written it in a book, so you just had to follow the rules about how meeting rooms should be laid out. If you were an account executive and there was a dead spot in a meeting, then you had to have a joke up your sleeve. Other rules set out what your responsibilities were, what you could and could not do. So I was amazed to discover, when I went to Saatchi & Saatchi, that the rules are a load of rubbish."

Like Tim Bell, Muirhead quickly fell under the spell of Charles Saatchi. "He's slightly like a bully, so you're a bit frightened," says Muirhead. "He makes you focus on the point all the time — 'Don't waste my time.' Everything has a speed and energy about it. It has to be done now or two minutes ago, and let's do it now. And he has the ability to galvanize people into doing things immediately." On one occasion, in the very early days, Muirhead was sent to the *Daily Mail* to sell them an ad he just didn't really understand or think was particularly good. It was a difficult task, but the paper's management loved it. When he got back to Golden Square, Charles saw the ad. "It's rubbish," he screamed, tearing it up in front of Muirhead before sitting down to write another. Nervously Muirhead returned to the *Daily Mail* with the new ad. They liked it even better than the first, and from that day on Bill Muirhead was hooked.

The Saatchi brothers were both painfully aware that for most large clients their agency would be considered simply too small. It was important to make the right impression, to present the right front, so when Singer, one of the biggest companies the agency was chasing, agreed to come in and see them, Charles was determined that the office should look right. The staff were told to call their friends and get them to come over. But it still didn't look busy enough, so Charles sent people out onto the streets of Golden Square to offer passersby a fiver just to come in and look as if they were working. That afternoon the office was full of admen, lorry drivers, and shop assistants. It was a typical Saatchi stunt. Singer was suitably impressed and the meeting went on well into the night. Charles, who was not involved in the presentation, got so bored he went home and changed, returning several hours later to discover the meeting still in progress.

By 1973 Charles was already talking to *Campaign* about his plans — highly ambitious for a three-year-old agency — to expand, even internationally. The first of many acquisitions was a small property company called Brogan Developers in 1972. This was followed a year later by the Manchester ad agency Dawes. Already the mechanics of acquisition that were to be used many times in the future were beginning to take shape. Companies were bought for an initial sum that included an earn-out for the managers; this meant they would receive final payment after an agreed period of time, usually between three and five years, but the amount would be dependent on the performance of the agency in the interim. It seemed like a good scheme, giving the current management every reason to keep their companies as well run and as profitable as possible.

Notley Advertising was acquired next, and then a company called George J. Smith. The latter turned out to be Saatchi's first big mistake: the company was ridden with debt and turned out to be worthless. Both were quickly absorbed into Saatchi & Saatchi, ranking them at number nineteen among big advertising agencies, with accounts worth a claimed, but perhaps inflated, £10 million a year. It was time to move to bigger offices, and Saatchi & Saatchi went to new premises on Lower Regent Street. By 1974 they were ready for the takeover that would change the fortunes of the agency forever.

Compton UK Partners was Britain's eleventh-biggest advertising agency, in which Compton Advertising of New York had a 49 percent share. In 1972 the company had gone public through a reverse takeover of a much smaller shell company, Birmingham Crematorium. The agency group had been sold to the crematorium for shares but took control of the new company and changed its name to Compton UK Partners. As a result of the deal, chairman Ken Gill found himself the proud owner of a bone-crushing machine, which he quickly sold off. But Compton had an uncomfortable year in 1974 as a public company in a depressed advertising market. Profits were down and shareholders were unhappy. The only solution seemed to be a merger between their main operating subsidiary, Garland Compton, and a smaller agency that would help boost turnover and profitability.

Saatchi & Saatchi was not Ken Gill's first choice. Originally he had chosen an agency called the Kirkwood Company, but his approach was turned down. It seemed Kirkwood's management were both frightened off by the huge task of turning around Compton's difficult position and afraid of risking their reputation with their own clients. Saatchi & Saatchi was not even second choice for Gill. In fact, his introduction to this brash young agency with its rather disreputable record for high-profile publicity came through an offer made by Maurice Saatchi to Compton's managing director, Ron Rimmer. Apparently the Saatchis were looking for a business manager and wanted to talk to Ron. He went to meet them, reported back to Gill, and within days Gill had decided he should talk to these brothers despite their unorthodox business practices.

As the negotiations developed, Charles and Maurice Saatchi began to realize what an interesting company Compton would be to acquire. At this young stage in its history, Saatchi & Saatchi had a strong reputation for imaginative advertising, driven by the kind of work it had done for the Health Education Council, but while it did have some pretty sizable clients, it had none in the really big league. Compton, on the other hand, had both Procter & Gamble and Rowntree Mackintosh. Ken Gill decided the time had come to talk to some of the company's most important clients and shareholders. The clients backed him. Milt Gossett, the fifty-year-old president of Compton in New York, reassured himself by flying to London to meet Charles and Maurice personally. His chairman, Stu Michell, took more convincing when he met the unorthodox Saatchi brothers, but in the end the deal went ahead. The Saatchis agreed to sell their agency to Compton for shares, owning a 36 percent stake of the combined new company. Compton in New York ended up with 26 percent, down from its original 49 percent. There was one last thing: the Saatchis insisted their name be kept. A compromise was reached and the newly merged agency, Saatchi & Saatchi Garland Compton, was born. The brothers bided their time until the last two names could effectively be dropped.

A reverse takeover of the holding company of London's Garland Compton agency in 1975 gave Saatchi & Saatchi a public listing. It also gave the company a feeling of ascendancy that, according to Paul Bainsfair, was not entirely deserved. "In those days, when they took over Garland Compton, Saatchi had the reputation of being a small hotshot, while Garland was considered to be an old, gray agency. In fact, when you compare the reels side by side, you see that Garland's work was actually better than Saatchi's — especially the TV work. Saatchi had two really good TV ads, for Jaffa and for *Cosmopolitan*, but Garland had all this glossy work for Nivea, lots of Procter & Gamble, not necessarily at the cutting edge of creativity, I admit, but really high production value — the sort of thing J. Walter Thompson is famous for — and I think people got rather a shock because it was much more a marriage of equals in terms of ability than you would have thought."

Ironically, one of the main casualties of the merger was Ron Rimmer, whose meeting with Maurice had initiated the talks between the two sides. Just after the deal was signed, Tim Bell announced he was to be the new managing director and Rimmer was to be financial director. It was not long until Rimmer departed for a rival agency, McCann-Erickson. His successor was the young Martin Sorrell, born in England and educated at Cambridge and then Harvard. He had initially met the Saatchis when he was working for a minority shareholder in Compton called James Gulliver Associates. His financial know-how was to have a huge impact on Saatchi & Saatchi's growth over the next ten years.

The deal was to be announced as a merger of two agencies.

But when *Campaign* led with a story headlined "Saatchi swallows up the Compton Group," there was a furor in New York. Once again Charles Saatchi had used his *Campaign* contacts to communicate his version of events. Some Compton people had already left before the deal was even officially signed, including the creative director and the media director, who decided to set up on their own. Saatchi & Saatchi moved out of Lower Regent Street and into Compton's offices on Charlotte Street.

While Charles and Maurice Saatchi were carefully secreting themselves away in plush new suites on the sixth floor at Charlotte Street, Tim Bell had his office on the ground floor. Occasionally he went to Maurice's house for dinner, though never to Charles's, and they often had lunch together. He even went to the brothers' parental home, but at heart he knew they never really accepted him as one of their own. "People in the company expected us to be closer than we were and saw the lack of intimacy as a snub," he says. "It was always Charlie who spoke to the press. He wanted to control it so journalists started to see me as a mysterious figure, the power behind the throne. It wasn't true. The whole third-brother thing was just a media myth."

To some extent, he was no longer taken into the brothers' confidence. And although he assumed the dual role of chairman and managing director in 1980, when Ron Leagas left the company, it was clear that his relationship with the Saatchis had deteriorated, and would continue to deteriorate as Maurice's long-term plan to acquire other subsidiaries necessarily reduced Bell's importance in the structure of the overall company.

Bell also felt that the company changed after the merger with Garland Compton. "The idea of a family may have been true of Golden Square and of Lower Regent Street, but it could hardly apply to Charlotte Street," he says. "At the very beginning it was a new company with a tiny staff of nine or so, and it had a very strong atmosphere. People were very competitive with the outside world. Perhaps any small business has a family atmosphere. When there's only nine of you, you see everyone all the time. When staff numbers rise to a hundred and fifty people, you don't."

But in those heady days, when new accounts were flooding in to the agency, Bell was on the front line and the rest did not seem to matter. Over the years many people have asked why Bell never went out and launched his own agency, especially in the boom years of the eighties. The former *Sunday Times* journalist Ivan Fallon, in his very sympathetic biography of the Saatchi brothers, says: "Most of those who knew Bell well say there is something incomplete about him, as if he could not function without the brothers, and Charles in particular." According to Paul Bainsfair, Tim Bell started to feel that he was no longer treated as an equal. "He used to say the brothers really took the piss out of him, never really took him into the thinking of the business. What he was expressing was that they are a close-knit Jewish family, incredibly generous and great bosses, but blood is thicker than water and there is no way that Tim would have been treated as an equal — and he resented that."

In its first year the newly merged agency underwent a complicated restructuring that effectively moved the American shareholders from the holding company to the operating subsidiary — in other words, the agency itself — giving the Saatchi brothers more control. The next year, the holding company was renamed Saatchi & Saatchi Company Ltd. This was the beginning of a confusion persisting in the public mind between Saatchi & Saatchi the advertising agency and Saatchi & Saatchi the holding company.

The early achievements of Charlotte Street helped smooth the way for further holding-company acquisitions, and as those deals became increasingly spectacular, they added kudos to the agency. According to the 1977 annual report, the agency had had a very successful first full year, with new assignments from a whole list of clients, including Black & Decker and British Rail.

In fact, this report makes very interesting reading. It talks about the Saatchi & Saatchi "belief in excellence." It says, "All our achievements are set by the 'norm' — whatever that is, by definition, there is a better way." With hindsight there is one particularly interesting sentence under the heading "Our Approach to Advertising": "We have never been believers in small agencies which are dependent on the style of one or two top men, however outstanding those individuals may be."

In the first year profits were just under £1 million and the company was still looking for fresh acquisitions. In 1978 Hall Advertising in Scotland was bought for £1 million, and the Dublin agency O'Kennedy Brindley was acquired two years later. A bid was even made, and refused, for Charles's former agency Collett Dickinson Pearce. New business was also rolling in, including accounts from British Leyland, Allied Breweries, and IBM. The agency was swiftly moving up the league tables. In 1976 the newly merged company had been at number seven; by 1979 it had deposed J. Walter Thompson from the top slot.

It was also around this time that some of the original staff started leaving. Ron Collins left ultimately to set up his own agency and Alan Tilby went off to direct television commercials. When Ron Leagas left in 1980 to start his own company after working under Bell as managing director at Charlotte Street, he was shown no mercy. "Initially the brothers couldn't believe I was going. They tried the old trick of sending for the checkbook and asking me to name my price. They even called my wife to tell her I had gone mad because I had said I wanted to resign. When they finally accepted it, I was cut off surgically. There was only the smallest of stories about my departure in *Campaign*. It was just like I was a member of a family who had married outside the family religion. You see, a very strong part of the company was the fact that people did not leave."

Paul Bainsfair compares the sense of loyalty that existed within the inner circle of Saatchi & Saatchi to the code of honor among Mafia families. "If you worked for them and they liked you, they gave you the impression they would do anything for you, and often did. They were very generous. For example, when my first child was born in 1988, they sent round a complete set of encyclopedias — really unexpected — probably worth a couple of thousand pounds — a fantastic gesture. Once, when I won an account, I got a message asking if I would like to stay at Charlie's villa in Italy for a couple of weeks with my family. You see, when something like that happened, you thought, he really thinks highly of me. But when I resigned, it was like I died — after all these things they had done for me — and in the first year or two afterwards I got the impression that if I saw either of them in the street, I would expect them to look the other way."

John Hegarty had also decided it was time to move on, as had Chris Martin. Charles took it personally and was so upset with Hegarty that he did not speak to him for two years.

"It's a great trick if you can pull it off," says a former colleague. "Because what it really says is, this company is more than a company — there is a specialness about it and we require a commitment beyond the normal. It works both ways: when you're there you feel you're working for a very strong, special operation, but when you leave it's like, what was that all about?"

To some extent, what it was about was the mysterious personality of Charles Saatchi. According to Hegarty, he is pathologically shy and very focused in what he does. "That's one thing about really successful people," he explains. "It's not necessarily about talent but about focus. People can be bright, but they also have to be focused, otherwise the energy is drained." To Ron Leagas, it started out as a sort of playacting, but the illusion turned into a reality. "It was an asset to begin with, and then he became something of a caricature of himself. It's a box that is hard to get out of — if you build up a myth, you might find actually Charlie is not that spectacular. In a business where people are only too pleased to stand up on a platform, or be quoted or photographed, it became distinctive and therefore a useful asset. Of course, it wouldn't have been any use if he didn't have the likes of Maurice and Tim and the others, who were able to say to big clients, 'Look, you don't need to see him.' "

four THATCHER'S ADMEN

*T*HE LEGEND OF SAATCHI & SAATCHI — the tale of how Maurice and Charles emerged from the traditional world of British advertising to become the pivotal figures in a luminous group of international message merchants and free-market hucksters during the eighties — takes its plot from the myth of Thatcherism. Legend and myth alike trace movement from the outside to the corridors of power, from tired conformity to vital iconoclasm, from social disadvantage to high society. So it is perhaps unsurprising how mixed was the reaction in 1978 to the news that the Conservative Party had hired Saatchi & Saatchi to run its next election campaign. Many in the industry were unimpressed with the winning of the Tory account. No agency had benefited in the past from being associated with a political party. Indeed, British admen had rarely taken political advertising seriously. Perhaps neither Charles nor Maurice could have foreseen how important the connection would later become to their business.

Tim Bell was despondent when he heard they had been appointed by the Tories. Ironically, the man who was to make his reputation running the account thought it would bring the agency nothing but trouble. He had been a young media buyer at another company when he had had his first experience of working for a political party and he knew only too well how disruptive the business could be, especially during election time. He also knew the brothers would leave him to sort out all the headaches, since they never handled accounts themselves.

Up until the 1959 general election, the Labour Party had spurned the trickery of the advertising business altogether, considering it an inappropriate way to publicize conviction politics. A young Anthony Wedgwood Benn was instructed by the party leader, Hugh Gaitskell, to supervise the making of party political broadcasts. It represented a significant change of direction, but in itself was not enough to defeat Harold Macmillan at the polls. Faced with a Conservative victory, Labour gave in to pressure and established a voluntary publicity group of advertising and public relations professionals to advise them in the future. The group was a success and produced some of the most memorable political slogans of the sixties.

The Conservative Party had employed a number of different advertising agencies, moving its account from one to another in the sixties and seventies and often using outside production companies for party political broadcasts. But during the seventies the Conservatives initiated a minirevolution by borrowing American techniques that included sharper camera angles and quicker cutting techniques to give them a much snappier feel.

In 1978 Saatchi & Saatchi was recommended to Margaret Thatcher by Gordon Reece, a former television producer who had been appointed head of communications at Conservative Central Office a few months before. He had come across Charles Saatchi in the sixties while making a commercial for the *Daily Mail*. When the newspaper's managers decided they needed some fresh ideas for their advertising they had called on Charles, and Reece had been suitably impressed by the unconventional young man.

Gordon Reece has often been labeled Margaret Thatcher's image maker, credited alongside Saatchi & Saatchi as the man who helped to transform her. Her hair was wrong, too suburban; it was restyled. The clothes were wrong, too fussy; they were replaced. The voice was wrong, too shrill; it was lowered in pitch through lessons from an expert on breathing. "Gordon loves a glass of champagne and fine cigars," wrote Cecil Parkinson in his autobiography, *Right at the Centre*. "During the 1979 campaign a senior official at Central Office raised with our Treasurer, Alistair McAlpine, the cost of Gordon's champagne and cigars. 'What does your car run on?' asked Alistair in reply. 'Petrol,' said the puzzled official. 'Well, Gordon Reece runs on champagne and cigars, and he runs extremely well on them!' "

By 1978 Saatchi & Saatchi already had a considerable reputation in the advertising industry. Known to be both creative and ambitious, it was no longer too small to be credible. Importantly, it was also a British-owned business.

When Charles Saatchi agreed to take the account, his brother insisted that the arrangement be put on a proper commercial footing. The Conservative Party would be treated like any other client, although the agency would obviously dedicate itself to the account during election time. David Puttnam recalls having a political argument with Charles as a result of the agency's work for Mrs. Thatcher. "It was so ridiculous. He might have been upset, but I was laughing about it," says Puttnam. "It was a row about the Labour Party. I'm a member and he is not an enthusiast. In fact, I think he is probably too right-wing for the Tories. He is idiosyncratic, with an idiosyncratic view of politics."

Tim Bell, however, soon reconsidered the client in a more favorable light. A committed Conservative, he was more interested in politics than either of the Saatchi brothers. Perhaps the account did have potential, he thought, perhaps it was worth the risk of one or two headaches. Bell went down to Conservative Central Office to meet the party chairman, Lord Thorneycroft, an old Etonian and a former chancellor of the exchequer in Harold Macmillan's government. While not particularly interested in the tacky world of advertising, Thorneycroft recognized that it was crucial for the party to have the right agency for the job. It rather surprised him that he took so easily to the charismatic young adman Tim Bell. And he recognized that the agency had a talent for direct, punchy copywriting that would be useful during the looming general election campaign. Thorneycroft was eager to get the work under way as quickly as possible and he charged the agency to come up with a party political broadcast for the following month.

Unlike in America, political parties in Britain are not allowed to buy advertising time on television. They are each allotted a certain number of minutes in which to broadcast their messages to the nation. Once again the brothers took an innovative approach by extending the principle of comparative advertising to a political campaign: the plan was not to talk up the Conservatives but to trash Labour instead.

Even while Charles was masterminding the phenomenal growth of Saatchi & Saatchi in the seventies and eighties, and even as he withdrew from much of the day-to-day work at the agency, he was always central to the campaigns the company provided for the Tories. His first efforts were sensational, with a film that showed the world moving backwards, from people walking backwards over Waterloo Bridge to climbers crawling their way down, rather than up, Mount Everest. Michael Heseltine appeared at the end saying, "Backwards or forwards, because we can't go on as we are. Don't hope for a better life — vote for one."

At the same time, Tim Bell was leading the agency's efforts to research voter attitudes. A team was sent to America to pick up extra ideas. Gordon Reece, who had himself worked in California, was influenced by the American system and was keen to import some of the techniques used across the Atlantic. The Saatchi team was also preparing its first poster campaign for the election.

In June 1978 Tim Bell made his first formal presentation to the leader of the opposition, Margaret Thatcher. He had a series of posters to show her, as part of Reece's plan to press ahead with a summer advertising campaign. "We decided to run our campaign in the summer," explains Lord Thorneycroft's old friend Lord McAlpine, then treasurer of the Conservative Party. "We knew in the summer there'd be no politicians about. They know nothing about advertising. They're a pain in the neck. Once they start rewriting ads, you have something that is four times as long and half as meaningful."

Andrew Rutherford, a member of the Saatchi creative team, came up with the idea for what turned out to be one of the most devastating political posters in British history. It featured a long and winding line of unemployed workers under the copyline "Labour isn't Working." Until then, negative political advertising had always been considered undignified, but Mrs. Thatcher loved the poster and the party went on the attack with it in August. In fact, the posters ran at only twenty sites, but this was enough to rattle the Labour Party.

The poster caused a massive furor. Government ministers were up in arms, and over the summer, when news stories were scarce, the controversy raged on many front pages. Denis Healey complained that the dole queue depicted in the poster was not a real one at all but was made up of a group of Saatchi employees. The Saatchis rejected the claim vehemently, although actually Healey had come dangerously close to the truth, because the people in the poster were really Young Conservatives. No matter, the free publicity was tremendous for the Tories, and Saatchi & Saatchi learned a valuable lesson they would use in the future: by writing advertisements that provoked Labour politicians into making public condemnations, their campaigns could gain valuable pages of free dissemination in the press.

Despite this success, the Saatchi people were still wary about their meetings with Mrs. Thatcher. "She'd invite you to a meeting, making it known there was no need for you to prepare anything, only to ask you what you had brought to show her once you had arrived," says a former member of the team. "Yes, she was autocratic, but she had endless common sense and she was the most consistent person I have ever met. She was relentless. It was impossible to have a conversation with her; she would just tell you things."

The Tory account marked the beginning of a close relationship between Tim Bell and Margaret Thatcher. A former Saatchi insider remembers how easily they got on. "Tim is warm, amusing, and very entertaining, she liked him immediately," he says, "but Maurice is none of these things. He can be charming, but Tim is naturally charming and the effect is to draw people towards him.

With Maurice there is a much more calculated effect." As the relationship developed, Mrs. Thatcher became maternal towards Bell. When she noticed he was looking a bit scruffy, she took one of his colleagues aside and told him to take Tim, as she always called him, to get a haircut. And she extended some of the same motherly concern towards others in the Saatchi team. Before her 1979 election victory, she invited some of the agency's senior managers to dinner. Jeremy Sinclair describes what happened when she unexpectedly discovered during the meal that he was a vegetarian: "She insisted I have some more peas, and continued piling them on to my plate. I told her I didn't want any more, but it didn't make any difference."

Saatchi & Saatchi was all geared up for an imminent election in September 1978 when Prime Minister Jim Callaghan announced he had decided not to call a general election until the following year. The team at Charlotte Street was hugely disappointed at the postponement, after all their preparations. Some even blamed Callaghan's decision on the impact of the "Labour isn't Working" poster, though in reality this probably did no more than contribute to an already unfavorable political atmosphere. Callaghan's decision proved to be a disaster for Labour. The following winter of discontent, with unions carrying out strikes to force through big pay raises and violent scenes on the picket lines, destroyed Labour's chances of holding on to power. Meanwhile Charles Saatchi, Jeremy Sinclair, and their team were busily rewriting the autumn campaign for the spring.

This would be the easiest election campaign that the Saatchis were to handle for the Conservative Party, fighting for the opposition against a weak and faltering government. A poster mimicking the "Labour isn't Working" ad was produced, showing a queue of patients trying to get into a hospital. Another had a child writing the words "Educashun isnt wurking" on a blackboard to play on the quite genuine concerns of people at the time about education policy. The next poster was even more direct: "1984 — what would Britain be like after another 5 years of Labour?" it asked.

Saatchi's TV work also intensified the campaign. The first broadcast showed runners racing around a track with the British weighed down with labels of "inflation" and "taxes." The imagery was crude and many of the party activists rejected it as too negative, but others thought it a strong, if overstated, attempt to capture the floating voter. A second broadcast showed stereotypical foreigners alongside an Englishman; while the foreigners collected money they had just won, the Englishman argued about the exact sum to which he was entitled. A third concentrated on the winter of discontent.

Each night during the run-up to the election, the Saatchi team reported to Conservative Central Office to hear the results of the latest polls, due out the next day. One evening the man from the research department appeared with bad news. Labour had been saying that the Tories would put up the value-added tax almost as soon as they were elected, and the public had believed them. Labour was four points ahead in the polls with only a week to go. Party chairman Lord Thorneycroft looked down the table at the nervous admen, doubting, perhaps for the first time, the wisdom of their strategy. "What shall we do?" he boomed. There was silence and blank stares; no one had the nerve to speak. "It's like this," he said. "You're in the ring. Your opponent has landed a punch directly on your nose and blood is pouring down your face. What do you do?" More silence. "There's only one thing to do now," he continued. "You have to land a blow on your opponent's chin that knocks him out." For Maurice this was a turning point. Lord Thorneycroft had confirmed Saatchi & Saatchi's instincts about political advertising. The agency and the party stuck to their guns. The attack on Labour continued unabated, the Conservatives trounced the Labour Party on polling day, and the Saatchis became famous all over Britain as "Thatcher's Admen."

"We do owe them everything, Charles and I," Maurice says. "When Mrs. Thatcher hired us, nobody had ever heard of us. Certainly not in America. That election victory in 1979 was the basis of our international — particularly U.S. — expansion. She was so respected in America that if she thought we were good, we were good. She made us."

The success of "Labour isn't Working" signaled a change in public attitudes to political advertising. Now the Saatchi team of writers, including Charles Saatchi and Jeremy Sinclair, became convinced it was almost impossible to produce effective political advertising without making reference to the opposition. Political advertising became more combative than any other form of advertising in the eighties. Once the Tories were in office, their advertisements turned the tables on Labour by treating them as if they were a failed government rather than an active opposition. In public, Conservative politicians deplored the negative advertising. They said they had plenty to boast about and wanted to be more positive. Party activists in the field were constantly sending their demands back to Central Office for a more positive campaign. But Saatchi & Saatchi knew the value of bad news, and the most famous advertisements they produced for the Tories were always the ones that talked about the real or potential disasters of a Labour government. "They had a wonderfully humorous way of knocking the competition," says Cecil Parkinson. "Their light touch led to ridicule rather than nastiness. I still find myself laughing today when I read some of their earliest ads."

Parkinson, the new Tory Party chairman, who got to know Tim Bell in the run-up to the 1983 election, is full of admiration for the Saatchi team. "They were the best, and everyone wanted to be with them. It was a honeypot of talent," he says. "Mind you, it was a long time until I met Charles. As a matter of fact, I used to say to Tim Bell, 'Does he really exist?' Because when Tim really wanted you to go for an ad, he would say Charles did this one himself. Charles occasionally wrote to me, and we did eventually meet for lunch at Wiltons. I thought he was rather like a human deer — charming, but tentative. He keeps his eye on you until he starts to relax."

The Saatchis quickly discovered that political advertising, unlike almost any other kind of advertising, has nothing to do with raising profiles. Political advertising is about getting people to like the politicians and their policies, while encouraging them to dislike the opposition's proposals. Jeremy Sinclair sums up the Saatchi strategy like this: "Our philosophy is to attack first. Attack. Attack. Attack. The retaliatory ads we did were great fun and the Tory Party allowed us to produce some of our best advertising. Even when they were in power we maintained the mentality of a marauding opposition. This was our instinct and I think it worked quite well."

As Saatchi & Saatchi grew in size and Maurice became more confident in public, he began to make a profession out of talking about political advertising. He would explain how simple messages had helped save the Tories during some of their most difficult years. "Simplicity is all," he said. "Simple logic, simple arguments, simple visual images." Saatchi & Saatchi's campaigns were so successful because they expressed the appeal of the Conservatives and the difficulties of the Labour Party in emotional terms, without getting distracted by the nitty-gritty of policy details. In a speech he gave in 1994, reprinted in the *Evening Standard,* Maurice explained his theories, carefully nurtured over the previous fifteen years: "If you can't reduce your argument to a few crisp words and phrases, there's something wrong with your argument. There's nothing long-winded about 'Liberté, égalité, fraternité.' Nor about 'Workers of the world unite. You have nothing to lose but your chains.' Nobody had to explain what it meant when they heard John Kennedy say, 'The torch has been passed to a new generation of Americans,' or Ronald Reagan describe America as 'a shining city on a hill,' or when they read on the Statue of Liberty, 'Give me your . . . huddled masses yearning to breathe free.' "

During the next decade the Saatchi strategy for the Conservative Party was simply "Oppositions don't win elections, governments lose them." In 1978 and 1979 everything was concentrated on the idea that it was time for Labour to go. Saatchi & Saatchi worked on the principle that a Conservative vote would be one for freedom, choice, opportunity, and prosperity.

The alliance between the Conservative Party and Saatchi & Saatchi turned the agency into a household name. Who were these two rather mysterious admen "Snatchy & Snatchy" or even "Thatchi & Thatchi'? Charles and Maurice themselves shunned the personal publicity, while allowing the agency to revel in its increasing notoriety. Charles, who had led the aggressive publicity campaign in the early days of the agency, recognized that fame, like success, would help attract new clients, but both brothers wanted to stay out of the spotlight themselves. It is ironic that despite the Saatchis' distance it was their name, rather than that of Tim Bell, that became inextricably linked with the Conservative Party. "Mrs. Thatcher thought Tim Bell was Saatchi's," says Cecil Parkinson. "I sometimes used to think she thought Tim did all the artwork and generally put things together, whereas Tim was the man who presented the work and explained it, and was brilliant at it."

Saatchi & Saatchi had its detractors. Some admen were jealous of the brothers' success and good fortune. As Margaret Thatcher's image and personal appearance began to change, the Saatchis were held to account for trivializing what was supposed to be serious politics. Labour was appalled at the way things were going. They tried to take some kind of moral high ground as they were beaten back by the aggressive attention they received at the hands of the Tories and their advertising agency. Who were these young admen who so persistently refused to come out of the shadows? The image of the hidden persuaders was resurrected by Saatchi's opponents. The brothers themselves were ideal targets because they were foreign. The verb "to Saatchify" entered the language as a new word for conspire.

As Saatchi worked wonders for the Conservative Party, so government expenditure on advertising began to take off. As the eighties progressed, professionals were increasingly called on, publicizing privatizations, preparing special announcements, even making an appearance in designing ministry logos. In fact, much of this political advertising was done by other agencies, for example, the campaigns for the privatization of electricity (the Frankenstein campaign), British Gas ("Tell Sid"), and British Telecom. Maurice Saatchi consistently defended advertising against those who thought that its use, particularly in the political arena, was immoral, favoring style over substance. He argued that only honest policies, or products, could stand the glare of publicity for any length of time. Advertising, he said, could speed up failure for a dishonest cause just as quickly as it could accelerate success for something worthwhile. He claimed that in a modern democracy advertising was one of the few mechanisms through which politicians could speak directly to the electorate without having their views filtered by media commentators and editors. "If somebody ever tries to tell you this is immoral, then ask them if it is immoral to comb your hair in the morning in order to put on your best possible face to the world," he said.

Meanwhile at Charlotte Street the distance between Bell and the brothers continued to grow even as Bell worked hard to create a good atmosphere. "Most of the people at Charlotte Street felt much closer to Tim Bell than to either of the Saatchi brothers," recalls one former employee. When Margaret Thatcher called a general election in 1983, four years after her first victory, it became clearer than ever to the Saatchis that he was now counted as one of the Prime Minister's inner circle. Maurice watched uneasily, worried that Bell was becoming too important, too indispensable. One former colleague described the brothers as "happy to devolve authority, but never power" ; they liked to be the ones in control.

The job in the 1983 general election was very different from the one in 1979. In the wake of the Falklands victory, Tim Bell assembled the Saatchi team to work closely with Cecil Parkinson, who by that time had replaced Lord Thorneycroft as party chairman. At her official country residence, Chequers, Bell showed Mrs. Thatcher a series of proposed posters for the campaign, but she rejected most of them out of hand. In the end Saatchi's came up with "Britain's on the right track — don't turn back," and she was delighted. "This was the first time I had seen Tim Bell in action on a major occasion with Mrs. Thatcher present," wrote Parkinson in his autobiography. "She clearly had tremendous confidence in him and he showed that it was not misplaced."

Charles Saatchi and Jeremy Sinclair wrote many of the ads that appeared during the three-way campaign. The first compared Labour's policies with the Communist Party's ideas and ran with the line "Like your manifesto, comrade." Other advertisements backfired. In one, the Tories offered a dozen bottles of claret (Social Democrat leader Roy Jenkins's favorite drink) to anyone who could outline the centrist Alliance's policies. Within hours of the posters going up, a group of Alliance supporters, carrying copies of their manifesto, turned up at Conservative Central Office to claim their prize.

Mrs. Thatcher rejected a great many of the ads Bell showed to her. "When she had said 'No' five or six times," Parkinson recalls, "I think she began to feel that she couldn't keep rejecting them, and then Tim would produce the one he really wanted her to consider, and, of course, the Prime Minister would say, 'This is better, Tim, this is better' — and this is where Charles came in. Tim would say, 'Oh yes, now Charles personally did this.' That, translated, meant 'This is the business, this is the one you cannot reject' — so there was this kind of unspoken code."

For the final week of the campaign, Saatchi & Saatchi planned a three-page advertisement — something that had never been tried before — to run in all the national newspapers, setting out the reasons not only why people should vote Tory but also why they shouldn't vote for the two main opposition parties. On the first page were ten reasons for voting Conservative. On the second, eight reasons for not voting Labour. The third page gave one reason for ignoring the Center. Mrs. Thatcher's immediate reaction was that the advertisement would be a waste of money. Thereupon Tim Bell replied that Saatchi & Saatchi would pay for the space itself. Cecil Parkinson, however, felt that the ad could be damaging to the party. "Even so, Tim Bell tried to waylay the Prime Minister because he really felt this advertisement mattered," Parkinson reports. "I said to him, 'Look, Tim, it's a bloody advertisement. You're not Michelangelo and that isn't the ceiling of the Sistine Chapel.' That is one thing you always have to watch with advertising agencies, of course. They're always looking to pick up two or three prizes for being the most daring, the most original. If you get too clever, it can be riveting for the rest of ad world but go straight over the heads of the public."

Bell had been running the Charlotte Street agency full-time, since successfully managing the merger between Saatchi & Saatchi and Garland Compton in 1975. While Bell had his office on the ground floor of the building so he could be at the heart of day-to-day events, the brothers had their offices on the top floor, close to Martin Sorrell, the finance director, who was working with them on the acquisition policy that was to take them to number one. There were constant rumors that Bell had begun to resent Sorrell, who seemed to have supplanted him as the third brother.

Today Tim Bell says he was relieved to be on a different floor from the Saatchis, having been caught up in the middle of too many of their fights in the early days of the company. He had seen enough chair throwing and temper tantrums to last him a lifetime, although, because he continued to vie with Maurice for Charles's attention and approbation, he continued to bear the brunt of some of Charles's most vicious outbursts. Bill Muirhead remembers one occasion when Charles was so angry that the physical force of his words alone were enough to drive him and Tim Bell back across the office. "Tim walked backwards in the face of all this abuse from Charlie until he was almost up against the wall, up against a work of art which had various bits of broken glass sticking out from it," he says. "Charles suddenly stopped screaming and ran over to Tim, telling him not to move. I'm not sure if he was more concerned about the picture or about Tim at the time."

The relationship between Charles and Bell was deep indeed — perhaps the deepest of the many relationships within Saatchi & Saatchi. But it was not, in fact, impervious to the brothers' jealousy. One former Saatchi insider says that the breach was the inevitable result of the evolution of a protégé into an equal, or even someone who had surpassed his mentors. "We all thought of Tim as the third brother, and he wanted to be a part of the family. What hurt the brothers was that Mrs. Thatcher became very fond of him, and in a way that made him bigger than them and they didn't like that."

Matters came to a head when Bell asked the brothers to vote him onto the board of the holding company and they turned him down. By this time he was no longer chairman of Charlotte Street. A year before he had quietly been moved into a new role as chairman of Saatchi & Saatchi Compton Worldwide, while Jeremy Sinclair had replaced him in London. Roy Warman, a former media director, and Terry Bannister, another long-serving Saatchi employee, were made joint managing directors of Charlotte Street — and dubbed the Pools Winners by some who could not believe their good fortune in landing the top jobs. During 1984 Bell spent much of his time advising Ian MacGregor, head of the National Coal Board, in the heat of the miners' strike, but he was still deeply unhappy and had to admit to himself that the time really had come to leave. Bell decided to team up with another adman,

Frank Lowe, head of a much smaller though rapidly growing agency, Lowe Howard Spink Marschalk. Lowe was offering him everything the brothers had denied him: his name as part of the agency's title, a position on the board, and equal status.

The parting was difficult and acrimonious. Bell concluded that perhaps the Saatchis had never liked him in the first place. Like those who had left the company before him, he was cut dead by the brothers. Today he has a more generous perspective on events. "Once you were not there, you no longer had any role in their life," he says. "Their whole lives revolved around the company. They chose not to speak to you because there was no occasion to do so. They just didn't keep up friendships with people after they left."

Mrs. Thatcher's relationship with Saatchi & Saatchi was never the same after Tim Bell left the agency. Although the situation did not reach crisis point during the 1987 general election campaign, the prime minister told the brothers — who had decided to run the campaign without Bell, even though he was still paid a retainer for his services — that in her opinion their recent work lacked bite. By that time Norman Tebbit had become party chairman, and Mrs. Thatcher had started casting around for fresh ideas. One of her speech writers, Geoffrey Tucker, introduced her to the London management of the giant U.S. advertising agency Young & Rubicam, which had already carried out a detailed survey of the government's ratings and its public standing.

One weekend in April 1986, the prime minister invited the Saatchi team to Chequers to hear their proposals for her next general election. As soon as the presentation began, the atmosphere in the room grew tense. Around the table were some of the Cabinet's most senior members, including deputy prime minister Lord White-law, Norman Tebbit, Chancellor Nigel Lawson, and John Wake-ham, the chief whip.

The Saatchi presentation was led by Michael Dobbs, later to become a best-selling novelist and the deputy chairman of the Conservative Party. Having previously worked in the research de-partment at Conservative Central Office, Dobbs had joined Saatchi & Saatchi after the 1979 general election because Mrs. Thatcher failed to offer him a job in Downing Street. That day at Chequers, Dobbs was assisted by another Saatchi man, John Sharkey, a bright young star at the agency but clearly lacking Bell's famous charisma. As Mrs. Thatcher looked around the table, contemplating the prospect of fighting her third general election, she was only too aware that many of the old faces who had helped pull her through before were now absent. Why couldn't she have Tim Bell to help her? Mr. Saatchi, as she insisted on call-ing Maurice, was just not the same, and her relationship with Norman Tebbit had already cooled.

In the weeks after the Chequers meeting, there was specula-tion in the press that the Saatchis were about to be sacked. Nor-man Tebbit took the unusual step of issuing a statement confirming that the agency would definitely be kept on until after the election. Tebbit demanded privately to know whether or not he had Mar-garet Thatcher's support; if he did not, he said, he was willing to resign. She said he had, and the conversation seemed to heal the rift between them.

As the summer progressed, campaign plans got under way and Saatchi & Saatchi started to gear up for battle. But Mrs. Thatcher was still unhappy. She was determined to consult Tim Bell. In response, Bell gave her his proposals for the entire strategy of the campaign and for communications across the board. Their meetings had to remain secret. "Maurice just did not have the same rapport with Margaret as Tim Bell had had," says Norman (now Lord) Tebbit. "Tim is a very good courtier, Maurice is not quite such a good one — and I am a very bad one. Tim had amazing charm. That is his strength and that is why he is such a good salesman."

The election campaign commenced, and Labour won plaudits for an unconventional party political broadcast directed by Hugh Hudson of *Chariots of Fire* fame, portraying Neil Kinnock as a family man, a leader, and a statesman. The opposition seemed to be out-Saatchi-ing Saatchi. At the same time, in a BBC interview, Mrs. Thatcher said that she hoped to "go on and on." Her opponents had great fun at her expense, adding that perhaps she thought she could go on, literally, forever. Bell was quietly summoned to Downing Street. Yes, it was true, he told her, Labour's campaign was stealing a march on the Conservatives, but she must be true to herself, follow her instincts, keep attacking Labour's policies. From that moment on, Tim Bell became a secret adviser. "I spoke to her every morning and evening and saw her with great regularity, because that was what she wanted," he recalls. "I leaned over backwards to agree with whatever she told me Saatchi's had said to her. I couldn't see that there was anything to be achieved by disagreeing."

Of Saatchi's posters in the campaign the most memorable one in the first ten days carried the slogan "Don't undo eight years' work in three seconds — vote Conservative." They got into their stride only after Neil Kinnock made a blunder on defense policy in an interview with David Frost. "What would the Labour Party do if the country was confronted by an aggressor with nuclear weapons?" Frost asked. Kinnock replied that it would not do to fight back, but occupation would be made as untenable as possible. Jeremy Sinclair and Charles Saatchi could not believe their luck. Overnight they put together the Conservatives' answer: a photo of a soldier surrendering with his arms in the air and the slogan "Labour's Policy on Arms."

As election day approached, the BBC broadcast the results of an opinion poll that showed Labour closing the gap at just 2.5 points behind the Conservatives. Rumors spread quickly through the City and share prices dropped. In many Tory circles panic set in. At the center of the storm, however, Norman Tebbit stayed calm. He had been consistently tracking the polls, which invariably showed the Tories well out in front. Nevertheless, Mrs. Thatcher would not be reassured. On "wobbly Thursday," as it became known, she secretly summoned Tim Bell to Downing Street. Bell and his partner, Frank Lowe, immediately prepared some ads to show to the prime minister. By the time the Saatchi team arrived the next morning, they were told that Mrs. Thatcher had decided to run with the Lowe-Bell ads. Saatchi's got the chance to rewrite them.

"The fact is the Tories won," says Bell. "And I think the last week's activity changed the atmosphere of the whole thing. It was a knockout blow, and it set everyone up to feel self-confident and it made the prime minister feel good. Up until then she had just felt demoralized."

In the days after Mrs. Thatcher's victory at the polls, news leaked out that during the campaign Saatchi & Saatchi's services had been as good as dumped in favor of another agency. A story in the *Times* even credited Young & Rubicam with saving Margaret Thatcher from defeat. Charles and Maurice were furious. They were particularly upset that Bell had been involved, as in their view he was trying to pass off their ads as his own.

Eventually a reluctant public peace was brokered, although in private the feud went on. For years afterwards the Saatchi brothers and Tim Bell refused to speak to each other. In order to avoid a disagreement in public, Maurice Saatchi gave the Conservative Party the opportunity to review its commitment to the agency by writing to the prime minister, "Saatchi has been moving into business areas which are bringing us increasingly into contact with government and government regulatory authorities. We are conscious that this might open the company, public authorities and ministers to misrepresentations." Mrs. Thatcher replied by paying tribute to the advertising agency: "We have worked together successfully," she wrote, "with the government carrying through policies which are right for Britain and with Saatchi presenting our policies skillfully and effectively."

Soon after the replacement of Margaret Thatcher by John Major at the end of 1990, the press was full of unlikely rumors that Saatchi & Saatchi was about to be reappointed by the Conservative Party. Maurice told the *Evening Standard*, "I was advised many years ago by a man who is now a senior Cabinet minister that you must never believe what you read in a newspaper unless you own it." But behind the scenes the agency had been working overtime to try and persuade the Tories to take them on for the next election campaign. Chris Patten, who had moved across from the Environment Department to the party chairmanship, declined to reappoint Tim Bell on the grounds that he was part of the Thatcherite "old guard." It looked as though Saatchi & Saatchi might be rejected for the same reason, until Bill Muirhead was dispatched to Central Office, where he managed to persuade

Shaun Woodward, a thirty-two-year-old former television editor now in charge of the Tory Party campaign machine, that since the average age at the agency was just twenty-six, many of its people had not even been working there at the time of the 1987 election.

Charles and Maurice were incredulous when they discovered that the agency had been reappointed by Woodward. Privately they had long ago written off any real possibility of working for the Conservatives during the next campaign. As a result, they returned with relish to the fray. As soon as John Smith, Labour's shadow chancellor, virtually ruled out higher borrowing, it became clear that there would have to be higher taxation to fund his spending plans. By the end of 1991 this had been distilled into the idea that a Labour government would cost the average taxpayer £1,000 a year more in tax, announced in Saatchi's "Labour's Tax Bombshell" poster, launched at the beginning of 1992.

The Labour Party, for its own part, was readying itself for the election. A Shadow Communications Agency had been set up by Peter Mandelson, the party's Director of Campaign and Communications between 1985 and 1990, consisting largely of volunteers from the advertising industry nominally headed by Chris Powell, the chairman of the advertising agency BMP DDB Needham. In order to obtain an outright majority, the Labour Party had to win more than ninety seats. The Conservatives were lavishing over £1 million on poster ads, carrying slogans such as "5 years' hard Labour" and "Labour's double whammy." Eight out of the nineteen morning conferences put either Labour's tax plans or economic recovery at the center. The Conservative campaign was attacked by party supporters, who were convinced that too much concentration on the issue of taxation would not help it to win the election.

On election night Maurice Saatchi threw a party at his London home for the entire Saatchi team, with the ads they had produced during the campaign lining the walls. Even as the party got under way there was still a general expectation in the country that there would be a hung parliament. At eleven-thirty it was announced that the key marginal seat of Basildon had stayed in Conservative hands. A former Saatchi employee remembers the wild scenes of jubilation in the room as it became clear that the Tory Party was heading for another term in office. "It was a crazy night, because we had been expecting to lose. And so Maurice hadn't invited very many people — it was like a wake, until the first results came through anyway — and then the place just went wild. I remember Charlie sitting at the piano and every time the Tories won a seat he played a sort of jingle that got more and more outrageous as the night went on." Towards the end of the night Bill Muirhead slipped out of the party and took a taxi down to Labour Party headquarters on Walworth Road. "I just wanted to see how I would have felt if we had lost," he said later. "It was just very quiet. People were walking round with their heads down."

In spite of the Conservatives' unexpected victory, the consensus among newspaper editors and columnists was critical of the Saatchi-led campaign. "The inevitable conclusion to be drawn from a Tory victory which defied the paucity of its campaign is that election advertising no longer matters — if it ever did," opined an editorial in the *Observer*. "The Labour Party pulled all the right poses but nobody was impressed by what was on offer. This is one instance where a failed product cannot be saved by better ads but needs to be withdrawn from the shelves completely." According to Lord Tebbit, Saatchi & Saatchi, however, did understand the difference between selling politics and selling soap powder. "They understood how the Conservative Party worked and the differences between working for a political party and for a commercial corporation. They also never tried to tell you policy. They knew they were not in the business of policy, just as, had they been working for Ford, they would have recognized they were not in the business of designing motorcars."

five   THE WORLD'S FAVORITE AGENCY

*L*ET US RETURN TO THE SCENE of the brothers ensconced on Charlotte Street in the summer of 1983. By chance, Maurice Saatchi happened to read an article in the *Harvard Business Review*. Its author, Theodore Levitt, was a Harvard professor of business administration and would later become an influential member of the Saatchi & Saatchi board. The article argued that it was no longer wise for multinationals to spend billions of dollars adapting and customizing their products for different international markets. National and regional preferences were on their way out. The secret now, according to Levitt, was to "globalize," to make a universal product, like Pepsi-Cola or Michael Jackson, that could be sold in exactly the same way throughout the world.

Maurice was spellbound by Levitt's ideas and very soon he was sharing them enthusiastically with one of the agency's newest clients, the inefficient state-owned airline British Airways (a well-known joke at the time had the letters BA standing for Bloody Awful). "Maurice is one of nature's great enthusiasts," says Jeremy Sinclair. "In fact both brothers are great enthusiasts. If you show Charles an advertisement, he will say it is either the best he has ever seen or the worst. Maurice, on the other hand, will just enthuse. If you watch people come out of his office, they are cheery and positive. If you've got a scheme, Maurice is a great one to be enthusiastic about it."

Saatchi & Saatchi had been signed up by BA the year before, at a time when the airline had just reported a loss of £300 million and John (now Lord) King had cut more than 20,000 jobs to prepare it for privatization. The agency was determined to promote BA without resorting to the usual airline advertising clichés of nubile stewardesses and catnapping passengers. In the course of his research, Bill Muirhead came across a helpful statistic — since British Airways had taken over many routes throughout what used to be the British Empire, the airline now carried more people to more destinations than any of its competitors. This led Maurice to his first global advertising idea. Saatchi & Saatchi would transform BA from the airline that promised "We'll take more care of you" to, literally, "The World's Favorite Airline."

The idea of "globalization" — it became Maurice's new buzzword — appealed to King. According to Cecil Parkinson, he was impressed by the Saatchis' ingenuity. "John King had a tremendous regard for Maurice," Parkinson goes on. "He thought Maurice was quite outstanding, a real hotshot, and took his advice on other areas of business apart from advertising. He thought Maurice was a very shrewd businessman as well as a clever advertising man and used to talk about him as one of the most impressive people he knew."

Saatchi & Saatchi's first advertisement for BA was a confident departure from anything the airline had ever done before. The commercial opened with an urban street scene at night — a dog being taken for a walk, a woman in her dressing gown standing by her front door, peering up at the sky as a large ominous shape passed overhead. The scene changed to an air traffic control room as a voice-over intoned, "Roger, Manhattan, continue to 2,000 feet." More and more people emerged from their homes. They stood gawking at the heavens as the entire island of Manhattan, blazing with lights like a giant flying saucer, appeared on the flight path for Heathrow Airport. The voice-over cut in again: "Every year British Airways flies more people across the Atlantic than the entire population of Manhattan."

The Manhattan commercial did more than globalize BA's advertising. It also reflected Saatchi & Saatchi's association with the confident new ethos of eighties Britain, fascinated by corporate identity, logos, and strategies. In the course of that decade advertising moved into the vanguard of popular culture. Soon it was being celebrated precisely because it sold the new, fashionable values of consumerism and, in other ways, embraced the entrepreneurial culture of the age. A later BA commercial dubbed "Red-eye" featured a businessman whose competitors had deliberately booked him onto an overnight transatlantic flight in the hope that he would arrive in no fit state for the next day's meeting. In the Saatchi scenario, however, the long-haul flight turned out to be so comfortable that the intended victim made it to his destination feeling rested and ready to do battle. It was as though British Airways — and by extension Saatchi & Saatchi — had become the champions, or superheroes, of the world's business travelers.

Yet not everyone at Saatchi & Saatchi was delighted to learn that the agency had won the British Airways account. Tim Bell, who heard about the deal from a third party, was devastated, especially since he had just led the successful bid to hold on to the advertising contract for BA's nearest rival, British Caledonian.

Clearly the agency could not keep both accounts; the conflict of interest would be too great. At any rate, that was how it seemed to Bill Muirhead, who likewise knew nothing of the BA appointment until it was confirmed. In fact, he had reassured his contacts at BCal that Saatchi & Saatchi was definitely not working for the competition. "When I got back to the office after a rather uncomfortable meeting at BCal I went to see Maurice to tell him about the rumors," Muirhead recalls. "But the minute I saw his face I knew they were true. Then Charles came into the room grinning broadly. 'Whyever didn't you tell us about BA?' I asked him. 'Well,' said Charles, 'we didn't want to say anything until we were sure. After all, there's many a slip 'twixt the cup and the lip.' " The brothers' clandestine maneuver was summed up by another Saatchi employee: "You've got to understand, these are not nice people," he said. "You can still love them and admire them. But they're totally manipulative."

Maurice Saatchi understood how globalization might be applied to Saatchi & Saatchi's own ambitious plans for worldwide growth. As far as he was concerned, Levitt's theory of global selling ought not to be restricted to products; it should also involve the agency's expansion into a global advertising arena. The brothers worked on the assumption that unless their company was one of the biggest in its field, it could never be really successful. Saatchi & Saatchi had to be in the Top Three. As they put it themselves, "One is wonderful. Two can be terrific. Three is threatened. Four is fatal." If the future lay in a giant global market, then of course Saatchi & Saatchi needed to have an office in every country. It was an argument based on economies of scale: bigger companies could afford to take bigger risks by investing in people and in resources to an extent that was out of the question for their smaller competitors. To put it simply, Maurice wanted Saatchi & Saatchi to be not just the largest advertising agency in Britain but the largest in the world — and it did not take him very long to set about realizing his ambition.

By 1986 Saatchi & Saatchi would acquire thirty-seven other companies, thirteen of them in just the previous year. "They wanted more than anything to be the biggest," Tim Bell recalls. "Always the biggest. I remember Charles screaming at Maurice on the phone, 'Get on with it, Maurice. Today's Monday. If you don't get on with it by Thursday there'll be nothing left to buy.'"

Everyone working at Charlotte Street agreed that it was Charles who was driving the company forward, while Maurice searched for ways to implement his grand schemes. The older brother had long since withdrawn from the day-to-day tasks of entertaining clients. As Charles grew more reclusive, Maurice began to emerge as a more confident, even more dashing figure in his own right. "I'm not as gregarious as Maurice," Charles explains. "Maurice can walk into a cocktail party and work the room; when I go to a cocktail party I stand in one spot in the corner and can't circulate and chat people up. In that sense Maurice and I are very different people. Maurice loves parties — he's that kind of chap — and gets on very well with almost anybody. He's got his faults, but he's easygoing and easy to talk to. I am less easygoing, less easy to talk to, and I'm not very good at parties, so I'm not your ideal clients schmoozer."

David Puttnam points to the advantages that accrued to Maurice from his brother's withdrawal from the limelight. "He became a very glossy and glamorous man," he says. "My daughter claimed he was the most attractive man in London." At the same time, Maurice began to entertain more and more clients or potential clients, hosting lavish parties at Old Hall, the mansion in Sussex, invariably with a guest list that boasted all sorts of celebrities from Cabinet ministers to pop stars. Lord Gowrie, former arts minister, now the chairman of the Arts Council, and a regular guest at Old Hall, has observed Maurice's self-effacing hospitality at close quarters. "Even when he is hosting one of his own parties, he is rather a quiet figure," Gowrie comments. "He's always a little bit at the edges of the party, slightly in the suburbs of his own city, and his movements are rather subtle."

According to David Kershaw, a Saatchi's account executive who rose through the company during the eighties and became chairman of the London agency in 1994, the brothers' motto "Nothing is impossible" and their undeniable contribution to the iconography of a glitzy decade served as a morale booster for everybody else who worked at Charlotte Street. "'Nothing is impossible' really meant 'Fuck it, we'll do it,'" he explains. "As soon as you'd broken one record, there was almost a cultural requirement to set yourself another ridiculous objective, prove the world wrong again." And in the mid-eighties the next objective, ridiculous or otherwise, was to seize the number-one slot in worldwide advertising by somehow acquiring another U.S.-based international network.

The Saatchis' restless ambition was beginning to make Milt Gossett at Compton Advertising in New York rather uneasy. He was worried that their world-beating philosophy was spinning out of control and predicted that sooner or later it would clash with the interests of large and precious clients such as Procter & Gamble. P&G, as it was known, liked to divide up its business and to keep its various agencies separate. Inevitably, there were rumors that the Saatchis had approached at least one other P&G agency in the hope of purchasing it. The brothers declined to play by the rules, and very soon Madison Avenue was awash with speculation about their acquisition plans.

Charles and Maurice started with tentative approaches to a couple of New York agencies, including Doyle Dane Bernbach, founded by one of Charles's heroes and one of the leading creative lights in American advertising, Bill Bernbach. They got nowhere, but Gossett heard of the talks and started to panic. He thought of attempting to increase his share in Saatchi & Saatchi Garland Compton in London in order to try to wrest back more control of the company, and he also considered forming an alliance with another U.K. agency on top of the Saatchi connection. Compton in the U.S. no longer had any share in the Saatchi holding company; its interest was purely in the London advertising agency. This gave Gossett a much weaker hand than he would have liked when bargaining with the brothers, but nevertheless he opened talks with them to see what they had in mind for the future of the company. First they suggested that Compton buy Saatchi & Saatchi, but Gossett said he needed time to think about such a big deal. Before he had time to reply, the Saatchis told him they had had a much better idea: they would buy Compton instead.

The idea was preposterous. Compton was still twice the size of Saatchi & Saatchi and much more established. Gossett decided that the only answer he could give the brothers was to buy another London agency and balance Compton's U.K. interests, and he hammered out a deal with KMP, a struggling agency ten years older than Saatchi & Saatchi. But Charles and Maurice were not to be so easily discouraged. Maurice approached Gossett again, this time with a formal offer. Gossett sat on the plan, although he could certainly see some advantages. Almost all his senior managers were reaching retirement age and he knew he would have to resolve the future of the company sooner or later. While they were still waiting for a reply, the Saatchis snapped up another agency in London. The acquisition was funded by placing £1.5 million worth of shares on the stock market. The scheme worked well and was to provide the blueprint for many Saatchi takeovers in the future. Saatchi's became one of the first companies to take advantage of the new money available during the eighties in the City — the banking establishment that had been so skeptical about the notoriously unpredictable advertising industry in the past.

Eventually Gossett signaled to the Saatchis that he was ready to begin talks with them. Charles was uncompromising — the Saatchi name must be kept in the title of any newly merged outfit. Its distinctiveness was a definite asset, he argued as the deal was finalized. The American firm could explain to the world that it was allowing itself to be swallowed up by the much smaller Saatchi & Saatchi only because it was easier for a public company to buy a private one than the other way around. (This was the exact opposite of the logic used to explain the original Saatchi & Saatchi takeover of Compton in the U.K. in 1975. In those days the public company, Compton, had been so worried about its position on the stock market that it had turned to a private company, Saatchi & Saatchi, to bail it out.) The Saatchis once again turned to the stock market to help them finance the deal, raising £26 million by using their favorite financial gimmick — a rights issue. This is a way of raising cash by issuing more stock, diluting the stakes of existing shareholders in the company in the process but offering them the "right" to buy enough new shares (generally at a discount) to still own the same percentage of the company.

Why Campaign is first

Campaign celebrates its second birthday this week with the inside story of the setting up of an important new agency. Over the last 12 months, in fact, all the major events of the industry have been recorded first and frequently only in Campaign.

At the same time Campaign's appointments pages, now designed in six columns, are carrying more job ads than any similar paper. The story is the same with display advertising.

More and more companies are realising that the best medium in which to advertise is Campaign. Because Campaign is the only publication to give a full, in-depth coverage of advertising and marketing

Home news 2-7, International news 8, Leader 11, Letters 11, Criticism/Press 13-15, Criticism/TV 16, TV Ratings 19, The Saatchi and Saatchi agency 21, Charles Marowitz on advertising 23, Campaign Interview—George Cannon of Alliance Cash and Carry 25-29, Advances 33-34, Appointments 35-43, Diary 44, Philip Kleinman 44

Ex-Pritchard Wood director goes to Eden Vale

BASIL HOOPER, a former director of Pritchard Wood, has been appointed marketing director of Eden Vale, the dairy foods subsidiary of Express Dairies. He replaces Fred Barker who retired in July.

Hooper, who joined Pritchard Wood after the Boase Massimi Pollitt breakaway in 1968, was in charge of account services and was thought at one time to be successor to Austen Barnes, then managing director of the agency.

But he left the agency in April last year following a top management reshuffle, when Barnes became chairman and was succeeded by account director Ian Pavitt and creative director Bill Jenkins. Since then he has been doing consultancy work.

Saatchi starts agency with £1m

CHARLES SAATCHI, the copywriting partner of the highly reputed Cramer Saatchi creative consultancy, is setting up his own agency.

It will start with five accounts and a billing approaching £1 million.

The accounts are Jaffa oranges, Granada TV rentals, the Health Education Council, a division of the Amoco oil company and a cosmetic and fashion company for which it will launch a new range of products.

Saatchi, 27, is starting the agency, Saatchi and Saatchi and Company, with his brother Maurice, 24, business development manager at Haymarket Press and a former promotions manager of Campaign. Maurice will be responsible for new business and "marketing the agency".

The agency is being backed by a City financial group plus a considerable investment from the elder brother.

The agency is strongly orientated towards the creative side and much interest will centre on whether it can be as successful as the Cramer Saatchi consultancy which is now folding.

For while admiring the work of Saatchi and art director Ross Cramer, critics have claimed that it is one thing to run a consultancy doing new presentations in a marketing vacuum and another to run advertising that must appear in the open market. Charles Saatchi points out, however, that he has produced campaigns, which have run, for a number of packaged-goods clients.

The Cramer Saatchi consultancy was formed over two years ago when Saatchi and Cramer left Collett Dickenson Pearce. Cramer will now direct commercials through the Terence Donovan production company (Hot Line, June 26).

The split appears to be an amicable one. Cramer, who will make most of the commercials for the new agency, says: "When it came to the point of forming an agency I realised I didn't want to go on working in an office for years. And I had become far more interested in the television side of advertising."

The consultancy specialised in presentation work for agencies and, according to Saatchi, worked for 15 of the top 20 agencies in London and helped move more than £6 million of billing. It became best known for its creative work for the Health

Charles Saatchi (left) and his brother Maurice ... on their own

Charles Saatchi : We'll cut ourselves off Page 21

Education Council, creating the anti-smoking campaign, the Pregnant Man ad for contraception, the award-winning Fly poster for food hygiene and the controversial venereal disease posters.

The consultancy also worked direct for a number of clients and, though the agency has not pitched for the business, it hopes that these clients will use it.

The agency will have three directors in addition to the Saatchi brothers: Tim Bell, 30, media manager at Geers Gross, a supermarket executive whom the agency will not yet name and a financial adviser still to be appointed. The group would consist of four creative

Two new creative people are joining those already at the consultancy. They are Ron Collins,

31, senior art director at Doyle Dane Bernbach, and Alan Tilby, 25, a copywriter at Collets. Collins will be an associate director with John Hegarty, an art director at the consultancy.

Collins was responsible for the famous Martell brandy campaign with French scenes such as an outdoor wedding reception, Dunn's suits which won the DADA ad of the year award in 1969, and Aer Lingus.

Tilby has worked on Hamlet cigars, the launch of Mellow Virginia Flake, Pretty Polly stockings and Ford.

The agency will have an unusual structure with working and control groups for each account. When a new account is taken on there will be a general discussion with all the staff after which a working group of six or seven will be appointed. The group would consist of four creative

TURN TO PAGE 5

Let the radio sponsors in, says Bow Group report

THE ban that prevents advertisers from sponsoring TV programmes should not be applied to commercial radio, says a report published today by the Bow Group, the independent group of left-wing Tories.

The report, prepared by eight Bow members including advertising and Press people, says: "If BP wanted to finance an opera performance in London and sponsor it on radio, a Texaco does with the New York Metropolitan, why forbid this?

Stations should carry a maximum of six minutes of advertising an hour, plus a speculation ration of time for advertising magazines of the shopping guide variety, says the report.

Commercial radio should be supervised by a Central Radio Authority operating through a Local Radio Authority in each station's area. Content should lie between "the pap and paternalistic extremes."

To help the bigger advertisers the central authority would have under it a central time-selling agency offering deals for national or regional coverage, says the report.

Authors of the report are David Weeks, a Benson account director, Donald Etheridge, marketing director of the David Macaulay agency; Max Hanna, an IPC marketing research executive; Pamela Dyas, an IPC research and development administration officer; Eric Reynolds, marketing executive at Sadler Wells; Terence Kelly, journalist and broadcaster; John Costello, a TV producer; and Patrick Hodgson, formerly of the Conservative research department.

Commercials firm to close down

THE Runnymede production company is to fold at the end of the month. Gordon Murray the commercials director and founder of the firm, says: "We have not gone broke and all commitments will be met when we stop trading."

Murray started Runnymede with lighting cameraman Stan Martin in 1959. In production the company turns this makes it one of the old established commercials shops. It has made films for Coca Cola, Dunlop, Philips, Ambrosia sago and the Dutch Dairy Bureau.

It was regarded as an efficient and low cost company but suffered from a lack of fashion image and a general slowing up of commercials production in recent months.

Saatchi & Saatchi kicks off with a front-page story in *Campaign*, London advertising's trade paper *(top left)*. Doing things in style was always important to Maurice Saatchi *(seated)* and his brother Charles *(top right)*. Jeremy Sinclair *(above)* was recruited by the brothers in 1968. Film producer David Puttnam and director Alan Parker *(left)* worked with Charles in the sixties, almost persuading him to become a screenwriter.

Tim Bell, seen here between Charles and Maurice in 1970 *(above),* jokingly referred to himself as the ampersand in Saatchi & Saatchi. The "Silk Cut Rhinoceros" *(below)*—from Charles Saatchi's favorite account—and the legendary "Pregnant Man" *(right).*

Would you be more careful if it was you that got pregnant?

Anyone married or single can get advice on contraception from the Family Planning Association. Margaret Pyke House, 27-35 Mortimer Street, London W1 N 8BQ. Tel. 01-636 9135.

7mg TAR 0·7mg NICOTINE
SMOKING CAUSES FATAL DISEASES
Health Departments' Chief Medical Officers

LABOUR ISN'T WORKING.

UNEMPLOYMENT OFFICE

BRITAIN'S BETTER OFF WITH THE CONSERVATIVES.

Their deliberately negative 1979 campaign for the Conservatives made the Saatchis famous as "Thatcher's admen." "Labour Isn't Working" *(above)*, one of the most devastating political posters of all time. Tim Bell with Margaret Thatcher on the roof of the Saatchi campaign head-quarters *(left)*. Thatcher developed a closer relationship with Bell than with anyone else at the agency, including the Saatchi brothers. In the closely contested general election of 1987, when Saatchi & Saatchi was handling the Conservative account but Bell no longer worked for the company, she called in Bell for advice.

Michael Heseltine *(top)*, who gave Maurice his first job, at the launch of a Saatchi campaign in 1992. Lord King *(below)*, former chairman of British Airways, "The World's Favourite Airline," whose corporate image was transformed by Saatchi & Saatchi in the 1980s. BA's defection to the new Saatchi agency in May 1995 — before it even had the name M & C Saatchi — was widely seen as punishment for the ousting of Maurice. Norman Tebbit *(left)*, as Conservative Party chairman during the 1987 general election, backed the Saatchis when they were being widely accused of running an ineffective ad campaign.

Maurice *(top)* with his second wife, Josephine Hart, whose novels *Damage, Sin,* and *Oblivion* have made her a literary celebrity. Charles *(left and above)* has for several years spent less time on advertising than on his other passions—art collecting and go-karting.

Maurice flanked by the men who later helped to depose him *(above left):* on his right, former chief executive Robert Louis Dreyfus, and on his left, Charles Scott, "the bean counter." David Herro *(above right),* the Chicago fund manager who led the shareholders' revolt. Tory Party chairman Chris Patten and chancellor of the exchequer Norman Lamont *(left)* unveil a Saatchi poster during the 1992 general election campaign.

IT COULD BE YOU.

THE NATIONAL LOTTERY

The Saatchi campaign for the National Lottery *(above)*. M & C Saatchi's controversial advertisement for British Airways *(below)*, developed in the New York office, provoked protests from American feminists. The new agency and its client claimed to be pleased with both the advertisement itself and the ensuing controversy.

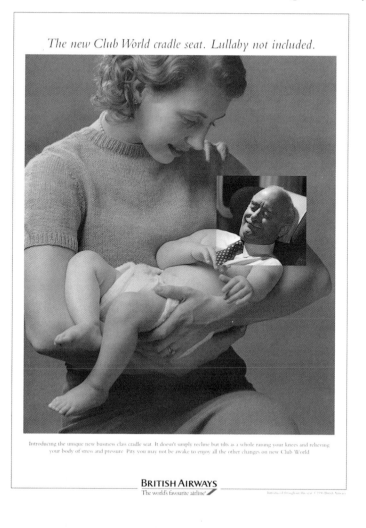

The new Club World cradle seat. Lullaby not included.

Introducing the unique new business class cradle seat. It doesn't simply recline but tilts as a whole raising your knees and relieving your body of stress and pressure. Pity you may not be awake to enjoy all the other changes on new Club World.

BRITISH AIRWAYS
The world's favourite airline

The "three amigos" *(above)* — from left to right, David Kershaw, Jeremy Sinclair, and Bill Muirhead—who resigned from Saatchi & Saatchi to help Maurice and Charles start the new agency. The London *Sunday Times* advertisement *(left)* run by the old company on January 15, 1995, as a morale booster following a week of top-level resignations.

The Compton deal announced in March 1982 marked an important turning point in the history of Saatchi & Saatchi. The financial arrangements meant that the brothers were forced to dilute their own holding from 36 to 18 percent of the company. Slowly the family firm was slipping out of their control and into the hands of unknown shareholders. However, they knew they had no option but to proceed if they were serious about expansion on the scale Charles envisaged.

The group they had purchased consisted of three parts: the New York advertising agency, the network of affiliated agencies around the world, and a group of companies that specialized in particular areas of advertising such as direct response and health care. The Americans received an initial $30 million as part of the deal, with the promise of a further $24.8 million over the next eleven years if the company's earnings grew in line with set targets. This system of up-front payments supplemented with long-term earn-outs had worked well in the past and was one the Saatchis would use a great deal in the future. Officially, as part of the deal, the Charlotte Street agency changed its name from Saatchi & Saatchi Garland Compton to Saatchi & Saatchi Compton London. In reality it made no difference at all, as the brothers made sure Saatchi & Saatchi was still called Saatchi & Saatchi.

In 1983 the brothers moved on to another round of acquisitions, using the earn-out scheme to purchase agencies in New York, Dublin, and Sydney. They were really on a roll when Saatchi & Saatchi got a stock exchange listing on Wall Street, only the third British company to do so, and at the same time they raised extra cash with a share placing for further acquisitions. The next year agencies in California and the Netherlands were snapped up. In the U.K. Hall Harrison Cowley and Hedger Mitchell Stark were also added to the Saatchi group.

In 1984 the brothers extended their globalization plans to include companies outside, though related to, the advertising industry. For years their clients had been asking them for advice on public relations, market research, and management; now the Saatchi empire would be able to provide services to answer all their needs. The first round of purchases took place in the U.S., where the acquisition of the New York research company Yankelovich Skelly & White was followed by the acquisition of management consultants the Hay Group, one of the most expensive Saatchi & Saatchi buyouts so far, with a price tag of some $80 million up front alone. But the company was an important addition to the group, with five thousand clients in offices scattered around twenty-seven different countries. Management consultancy was a growing business and the Saatchis were confident they could make a success of it. In 1985 Saatchi & Saatchi's buying spree accelerated, with businesses outside advertising being acquired at the rate of one a month. They were still gobbling up advertising agencies too. The purchase that year of the Rowland company propelled them into the public relations field, and other PR companies followed. Robin Wight, head of Saatchi rival WCRS, remembers the Saatchis as being "like the Japanese coming over the trenches on those death beaches in the Pacific. They took no prisoners. And they pulled every bloody string."

Following their great flurry of acquisitions, the Saatchis decided that the business should be split in two: Saatchi & Saatchi Communications, comprising the advertising companies, and Saatchi & Saatchi Consulting, headed by Milton Rock of the Hay Group. Maurice had already begun to search for a troubleshooter who would be able to shape the advertising businesses into some kind of manageable structure. He consulted a firm of headhunters who suggested Anthony Simmonds-Gooding, then chief executive of the Whitbread brewing company. Immediately Maurice, who was convinced that he had found the right person for the job, set off in pursuit. It is hardly surprising that Simmonds-Gooding was bowled over by the Saatchi charm. He told colleagues later that Maurice had been so determined to hire him that it was as if the world-famous adman had climbed up the drainpipe with a red rose between his teeth in order to seduce him into submission. Yet Simmonds-Gooding quickly discovered the other side to the Saatchis' delight in the grand gesture. When he arrived for work on his first day, he found that the brothers had gone off on holiday for two weeks, leaving him to hold the fort in what turned out to be a peculiarly difficult situation.

The new chief executive was the first person the Saatchis had ever employed to stand between them and the managers of their advertising agencies. He soon realized that knocking the miscellaneous companies into shape would be no easy task. Yet his appointment enabled the Saatchis once again to direct their attention to Madison Avenue — and this time they had their eyes on the biggest prize of all.

Ted Bates was the world's third largest agency. Its greatest days might have been over, but Bates was still a very special company in the minds of those who worked in the advertising industry. Its founder had developed his own advertising theory known as the unique selling proposition, or USP. The idea of USP, by now an accepted part of advertising jargon in London as well as New York, was that every advertisement should demonstrate that the product it was advertising could offer the consumer a single clear benefit not available from any of its competitors. The Saatchis wanted Bates so desperately they were prepared to pay $300 million. Bates asked for $450 million. The brothers reluctantly agreed and set up yet another rights issue to raise the necessary money.

The Saatchis merged Ted Bates with another expensive and recent American acquisition, the Backer & Spielvogel agency (which cost them $100 million), and called the new conglomerate Backer Spielvogel Bates Worldwide. Now Saatchi & Saatchi PLC was a vast holding company with advertising agencies, management consultancies, and media-buying companies within the group. At last it was the biggest advertising company in the world.

In 1988 David Ogilvy published an updated edition of his famous book *Confessions of an Advertising Man*. Predictably, as an adman of the old school, a man who valued the craft of advertising above the practice of corporate wheeling-and-dealing and hostile takeovers, he condemned the Saatchi & Saatchi style of empire building. In a revised afterword, Ogilvy lamented what he called "the emergence of megalomaniacs whose mind set is more financial than creative. They are building empires by buying up other agencies, to the consternation of their clients. Haven't they ever heard of the South Sea Bubble?"

By the second half of the eighties the Saatchi bubble was about to burst. The Bates deal, planned as yet another magnificent coup, quickly turned sour. Some of the agency's biggest clients were appalled that the company was now in the hands of the notoriously ambitious Saatchi brothers. Forrest Mars, head of the Mars Corporation, told them he would review his company's entire $200 million account. Other clients followed suit. Colgate Palmolive withdrew $80 million worth of its budget, and Warner Lambert — spending an estimated $68 million a year — also told the management of Bates that it was considering terminating its contract with the agency.

In 1995, at the end of his career with Saatchi & Saatchi, Maurice Saatchi cast himself as the defender of clients and the guardian of their interests. He condemned those who had plotted against him, those who had ignored the wishes of powerful clients, among them the very same Forrest Mars. "I have watched in dismay as some of our longest client relationships have been jeopardized, the wishes of key clients ignored, and the loss of their business assessed as a 'price worth paying,'" he wrote in his resignation letter. Yet a decade before, he and his brother were only too willing to ignore their clients' concerns if they stood in the way of Saatchi & Saatchi's rampant expansion. Procter & Gamble, their most important client, had told the brothers that it would not tolerate the agency working for any of its rivals. But with the purchase of Bates, just such a rival, Warner Lambert, was now part of the client list. Maurice was forced to fly to P&G's headquarters in Cincinnati himself to try to sort out the problem. In the end they removed just one small account, but Maurice was left in no doubt that everything the company did from now on would be closely scrutinized. Saatchi & Saatchi was on probation. Maurice was less successful with other unhappy clients, as Bates continued to hemorrhage business. Three months after the deal had been agreed, Michelob, McDonald's, and Nabisco had all walked out. Mars and General Mills stayed on, but when Maurice visited them he was given a frosty reception. To add to the troubles, Backer & Spielvogel and Saatchi & Saatchi had also started to lose accounts, as part of a damaging domino effect. By mid-August the group had suffered account losses worth close to $359 million. There had been some gains too, but the overall results of the deal were proving devastating to the two brothers who had only ever tasted success.

The Saatchi share price tumbled at news of the Bates difficulties. Rumors about the $100-million handout paid to Robert Jacoby, chief executive and part owner of the agency, only added to the furor. How could anyone in the advertising industry deserve such a large sum? These Saatchi companies must be overcharging their clients to be able to afford it, competitors speculated. Maurice and Charles started to round on Jacoby, who was still reporting for work. The brothers had assumed that the $100-million payout would guarantee Jacoby's hard work and dedication through a difficult period. But this aspect of the acquisition scheme turned out to be a costly mistake. As far as they could see, Jacoby had just taken his cash and watched events unfold. The Saatchi brothers' clever earn-out policy, so carefully devised with Martin Sorrell, was coming apart. The Saatchis knew how to buy companies; what they didn't know was how to merge them. Much later, Maurice Saatchi was forced to admit that the policy that had worked well for the company in the seventies and early eighties contained a fatal flaw. The earn-outs gave previous owners of companies an incentive to maximize the profitability of their agencies only over a short period of time, just until they got their payoff. Many pared costs to the bone, stripping the companies bare of any resources. Profits went up in the short term, then managers took their money and ran, all too often leaving behind them an empty shell.

"The Saatchis were motivated by money and always thought other people were too," says one former colleague. "They wanted to buy people who worked for them cars, holidays, swimming pools, even houses. They were very generous, but the less you asked for, the more paranoid they became."

There was worse to come. Internal strife arose at Bates between Jacoby and two of his senior managers, both in very influential positions with important clients such as Procter & Gamble and Mars. P&G was the first to snap. Enough was enough. The Saatchi brothers had to be taught a serious lesson. P&G withdrew $85 million worth of its advertising from Saatchi & Saatchi Compton in New York.

Anthony Simmonds-Gooding, still trying to find a new structure for the endless number of Saatchi companies acquired during the brothers' frenzied buying spree, was told to sort it out. He went to see Jacoby and informed him that he was planning to merge the agency with other Saatchi group companies. The turmoil could not be allowed to continue any longer; he would deal with the management trouble at Bates himself and Jacoby would have to accept a new job somewhere else in the Saatchi organization. In the end Jacoby quit, successfully suing Saatchi & Saatchi for breach of contract.

Wall Street was appalled, and Simmonds-Gooding came under renewed pressure from the brothers to find a workable structure for the communications division. Initially he favored the idea of one giant merger, putting everything together under the Saatchi & Saatchi name. It was an ambitious, perhaps even visionary, plan. But realistically he knew it could never work. One giant operation would have been an organizational nightmare. P&G warned Saatchi that it would not allow the agency to move its account anywhere near the Bates company; the brothers knew that P&G had had just about as much as it could take. Simmonds-Gooding completed work on a second plan by June 1987, merging New York–based Dancer Fitzgerald with Saatchi & Saatchi Compton to form Saatchi & Saatchi Worldwide (the London agency Dorland was left out of the deal as a stand-alone operation). By then, however, Simmonds-Gooding had had enough. He had created some order from the mess he inherited, and it was with relief that he left the Saatchi empire later that year. By the end of 1987 the financial community had begun to recover its confidence in Saatchi & Saatchi, reassured by another set of satisfactory quarterly results. But part of the Saatchi magic had gone. Martin Sorrell had left the company before the Bates deal was negotiated and some in the City began to be suspicious that, without his steady hand, the Saatchi brothers were in danger of taking the company off the rails. Even so, the restless Saatchi gaze was shifting to bigger and more ambitious projects.

The brothers Saatchi never managed to export their shining U.K. reputation as the world's most famous and best-loved admen across the Atlantic. In the U.S. the Saatchi story had been interpreted very differently. Charles and Maurice Saatchi were not perceived to be the visionaries of the advertising industry that many in Britain believed them to be. Instead, as they expanded their business interests in a deeply conservative American ad industry, they were frequently termed the unscrupulous foreigners, who in the boom years of the 1980s had come across the seas to lay siege to some of America's longest-established advertising agencies, buying them up in an acquisition frenzy and then dismembering them and merging them with other businesses in a process that saw some of Madison Avenue's most famous names disappear forever — Compton Advertising for one, Ted Bates for another. In

1987, when the brothers decided to consolidate their U.S. agencies into two giant advertising networks, Saatchi & Saatchi Worldwide and Backer Spielvogel Bates, the resentment in New York was almost palpable.

The Saatchi shopping spree was equally unpopular with the clients of their new American agencies. Some, who had been loyal to their advertising agencies for years, suddenly found themselves, to their horror, shunted into one or the other of the two new Saatchi networks alongside their direct competitors. The subsequent fallout was devastating as major big-spending clients demonstrated their disapproval and went elsewhere — Colgate Palmolive and Warner Lambert were only two of the biggest. The old stability in the U.S. advertising industry was gone forever, and many, including *Advertising Age,* blamed the actions of Saatchi & Saatchi for the ensuing insecurity: "The string of ad agencies Mr. Saatchi acquired was upsized, downsized, combined and dismantled — to the point where the traditions and stability of the business no longer existed," it observed.

When times had been bad in the U.K., the Saatchis had always been able to rely on the strength of their creative reputation to pull them through. The quality of the work produced by their agencies earned them an enviable reputation in London's Adland and gave many industry insiders an excuse to overlook some of their early business blunders. The brothers were not so fortunate in the U.S. There had of course been exceptions, such as the award-winning Lexus campaign produced by Saatchi's West Coast agency, with the slogan "The relentless pursuit of perfection." But on the whole the Saatchi name did not stand for inventive advertising in the U.S., as it did in the U.K. Other well-known campaigns, such as the "Miller Time" ads for Miller beer, were indeed done by Saatchi agencies, but before they had been acquired by the brothers. In the early eighties Bates had also created the memorable "Tastes Great — Less Filling" ads for Miller Lite, only to lose the account in 1991. Other good work was being done by Bates for car client Hyundai, with one well-remembered ad showing a man trying to drive two cars to illustrate that, because they were such good value, it was possible to buy two for the price of one. "While Charles was respected as a creative adman in the U.K., he had never worked in the U.S. and Americans did not feel the same about him or the work of the Saatchi agencies," says an insider. "Maurice was regarded as a naive businessman who was taken for a sucker in some of the prices he paid to acquire agencies."

But there was more behind the American bad feeling towards Charles and Maurice than their seemingly insatiable appetite for the cream of U.S. advertising institutions. As the brothers showered literally millions of dollars in sweeteners on the existing managers of their newly acquired stateside advertising agencies, the repercussions of one gigantic handout after another were felt across the whole industry. Appalled at the amounts of money being dished out, clients erupted into a fury, demanding to know how agencies such as Saatchi & Saatchi had managed to generate huge profits, unless it was at their clients' expense.

"It was the end of an era for American advertising agencies," said one former Saatchi manager. "The size of the Saatchi acquisitions told clients how much money agencies were making out of them and led to clients demanding better deals. No one in American advertising was going to forgive the Saatchi brothers for opening up that particular can of worms."

The advertising business had been run for years on a commission system that traditionally entitled agencies to 15 percent of their clients' advertising budgets. Now these levels started to plunge, as clients adopted a new get-tough attitude. When the advertising recession hit, in the late 1980s, many agencies found they could not survive on their revised, lower levels of income, and many blamed the squeeze on the extravagance of the Saatchis.

Saatchi & Saatchi had expanded into much more than just an advertising business. It owned companies in management consultancy, corporate image, public relations; in fact, its companies covered a whole range of marketing activities. Saatchi & Saatchi was a service organization with something to offer to the banking sector — which in Britain desperately needed to smarten up its record on servicing its customers. Midland was the ideal target. Once one of the biggest banks in the world, it was now in trouble, heavily burdened with Third World debt, against which it had had to set aside a reserve of £1 billion. Nevertheless, the bank's name remained very prestigious.

Speculation began in September when tycoon Lord Hanson started buying up shares in Midland. Maurice concluded he must move quickly to stand any chance of success. Such an acquisition would cost between £3 billion and £4 billion, the Saatchis estimated, as they canvassed friends in the City to ask for their advice. Maurice met with Treasury officials and senior managers at the Bank of England. At last he arranged a meeting with Kit McMahon, Midland's chairman, in order to advance his well-rehearsed arguments on globalization. McMahon was skeptical about an advertising agency's ability to run a bank, but he was still willing to listen to Maurice's proposals with an open mind. All was going smoothly until McMahon asked Maurice about his ideas on the bank's bad debts in South America. Maurice, out of his depth, blustered. He said he thought the bank had already taken care of the debt — and with that single mistake he destroyed his credibility with McMahon. He knew immediately that he had blown the deal. As a result, Saatchi & Saatchi stock tumbled. "It became a cause célèbre," Maurice says. "People thought, these upstarts reached too far — they're too big for their boots. 'Jumped-up Adman Seeks to Buy Noble Banking Institution' — it writes itself, doesn't it?"

In retrospect Charles Saatchi admits that the Midland Bank project was a fiasco from beginning to end. Yet the brothers were misled by the apparent ease with which the necessary financing was agreed. "All the froth in the City meant anyone could do anything, so it wasn't hard to find money available to buy Midland Bank," he adds. "It sounds daft now, I know. Back then, when people were doing such megadeals, it wasn't so daft. The bank was incredibly cheap, just as an opportunistic deal. We thought, 'Let's suck it and see,' so we got the money and had one meeting with Midland Bank, at which they told us to piss off — and that was it."

Cecil Parkinson agrees that the Midland Bank affair is often misunderstood. "Hindsight is a mixed blessing," he says. "And it's hard perhaps to remember how dominant the Saatchis were at one stage. No one at the time regarded it as a joke when they went to Midland Bank with a plan to take it over. Of course, it was an amazingly self-assured thing to do, but at that point virtually anything they touched turned to gold and it seemed quite reasonable for them to have this kind of ambition. They had such a reputation at the time, they were so preeminent, such market darlings, that people thought they must have known what they were about."

But even before the management of Midland Bank had formally rejected their overtures, the Saatchi brothers had shifted their sights yet again, this time focusing on the merchant bank Hill Samuel. Initial talks seemed to go well, but the financial press was derisive and so the Hill Samuel project was quickly abandoned. "There is a lesson we can all learn from the Saatchis' act of folly," says Norman Tebbit. "When each of us goes home at night we should look in the mirror and say, 'Am I as clever as I think I am, or have I just been lucky so far?' There's a time when you should look at the chips left on the table and say to yourself, 'That was a great game, I enjoyed it, now it's time to walk away.'"

The eighties came to an abrupt end with the stock market crash in October 1987. The loss of confidence was devastating, although Saatchi & Saatchi managed to hold on in the short term, with its profits continuing to surge ahead. "At the time the crash didn't seem so terrible because it was happening to everybody," says Paul Bainsfair. "It just wasn't clear then that there would be no recovery for Saatchi & Saatchi. The only thing that really concerned us was the fact we all had huge share options which were becoming more worthless by the day. Having grown up at Saatchi's meant you were used to a certain amount of aggressive bad publicity. People look back and say they were fated, but at the time we were regarded as a huge success story. But within the context of the advertising industry they were always slightly positioned as outsiders and hype merchants."

In 1988 Saatchi & Saatchi was still the biggest advertising group in the world. Three years later, its shares had lost 98 percent of their value and the company was no longer number one. In fact, it had been overtaken not only by WPP — now comprising J. Walter Thompson and Ogilvy & Mather, under the directorship of

Martin Sorrell — but also by the American companies Interpublic and Omnicom. "I think people thought we could walk on water," says Maurice. "The evidence appeared to be that we could. But our timing was exquisitely bad, because in 1990 the advertising market fell, in nominal terms, for the first time since the war. People had very nice computer models of advertising growth continuing. But it didn't."

The brothers decided that the future lay not in the advertising but in the management-consulting end of the business. At the beginning of 1988 they had taken on Victor Millar, the second in command at Anderson Consulting. Initially he was employed as head of both the consulting and the communications sides of the company, but he soon moved across to manage consulting alone. Two of Charlotte Street's protégés, Roy Warman and Terry Bannister, were moved up to the holding company to take charge of communications. Anthony Simmonds-Gooding had masterminded the new structure, but agencies were still being thrown together and few of the mergers were being managed at all.

The crunch came finally in 1989, with the first-ever profits warning to investors. Costs were still spiraling and a new austerity program was introduced. The company could not cut costs fast enough. The reorganization and staff reductions that year led to an exceptional charge of £29.5 million. After so many years of continuous growth this was a blow indeed. Many of the advertising agencies had been bought during the mid-eighties at a time when advertising was booming. Now the market went into one of the worst slumps since the war. "The very worst moment of my career," said Maurice Saatchi later, "was having to stand up in 1989 at the annual general meeting — after eighteen years of consecutive profit growth — and say that we were not going to meet our profit expectations for that year." The company announced that it was putting an end to the growth of the consulting division. That fiscal year alone, three businesses were sold off, but under conditions the announcement itself had rendered catastrophic. Once the market realized that Saatchi wanted out of consulting, the result was a fire sale in which companies went at rock-bottom prices. Overnight Victor Millar's job changed from acquisitions to disposals and Warman and Bannister were left running what had become a single-division company. Some of the earn-out deals from previous years were maturing, and Saatchi & Saatchi was scrabbling to find the cash to meet them as the recession hit harder and debts mounted. Worse, in 1988 the brothers had been persuaded to raise money by means of a new kind of share offer called the Euro-convertible — if the stock price failed to rise above 441 pence by mid-July 1993, the company would be obliged to buy back the shares at the original price plus a 20 percent bonus. With the current catastrophic fall in Saatchi & Saatchi shares, the company was left facing a £200 million payout to Euroconvertible holders.

The Saatchi brothers were forced to admit to the world that they were incapable of sorting out the problems, and to start to look for someone else to come in and take control.

Looking over their shoulders, it must have been galling to watch the success of Martin Sorrell, another Charlotte Street protégé and the man whom David Ogilvy had famously dismissed as "that odious little jerk." In due course, however, Sorrell also fell victim to the slump in the advertising business, and by 1990 his company too was publishing a profits warning as its share price collapsed. It is hard to know whether the Saatchi brothers derived any comfort from the misfortunes of a former colleague who had likewise overreached himself. In any case, Charles Saatchi is nowadays philosophical about the catastrophic events that marred the earlier triumphs of Saatchi & Saatchi in a helter-skelter decade.

"We made all kinds of screwups after a fantastic run," he recalls. "We just did not foresee a downturn, and when we wanted to make a big leap forward it didn't work. Things turned very sour after the Midland affair. The crash came, and then the recession, and we were never able to recover."

six BUSTED FLUSHES

SAATCHI & SAATCHI HAD EXPERIENCED almost two decades of uninterrupted growth. Now, in the aftermath of the Midland Bank affair, the brothers' credibility with shareholders and the City was in tatters. By early 1990 Saatchi & Saatchi PLC was on the verge of bankruptcy. Charles realized that the company required emergency treatment. "We were busted flushes," he says frankly. "The City thought we were complete idiots. Our staff thought we were idiots. So we said to ourselves, 'We've fucked up — let's go and hide in a corner.' Don't forget, there were clients who still liked us. At that stage the easiest thing in the world would have been to leave. We'd already sold most of our shares. We could have walked away and perhaps come back with another business. But we couldn't do it. There were too many people we loved at the agency, and Maurice is very popular with clients — it doesn't matter whether I think he's a jerk or not. In any case, we wanted someone to solve the problem."

As soon as Charles had admitted to himself that the company's troubles were out of control, he pressed Maurice to find a new chief executive who could save it from total collapse. "My brother is brutally frank on many subjects," says Maurice, who until then filled the roles of both chairman and CEO. The brothers concluded that the only way to reassure the City and Wall Street was to bring in some professional managers.

Robert Louis-Dreyfus was not Maurice's first choice. He had approached London Weekend Television's Sir Christopher Bland and two others before turning to a Pennsylvania-based company called IMS, which specialized in supplying research data to pharmaceutical firms, and which had once been the target of their own ambitious acquisition plans. The company's chief executive, Louis-Dreyfus, a Frenchman, became the new Saatchi chief executive, bringing with him Thomas Russell as a nonexecutive director and IMS finance director Charles Scott.

The man hired by the Saatchi brothers to rescue their ailing advertising group from bankruptcy was a mystery to the rest of the London advertising world. Louis-Dreyfus had no experience in advertising. He was an old-fashioned playboy who had been linked in the gossip columns with Kim Basinger. Drawn to Saatchi & Saatchi by its glamorous image and the opportunity to save the most famous advertising agency in the world from collapse, the new chief executive was obviously not taking the job for its £500,000 salary alone. Robert Louis-Dreyfus in fact hailed from one of the richest families in Europe. The family's fortune had been founded in the nineteenth century in the small Alsatian town of Sierentz by one Leopold Dreyfus. At fifteen, Leopold wheeled barrows of grain from his hometown across the border into Switzerland, where it fetched a higher price. Since it was illegal in French law for anyone under the age of twenty-one to own a business, Leopold used the name of his father, Louis. The business prospered, and when he came of age Leopold altered his own name to Louis-Dreyfus. Towards the end of the century the family extended its business interests into new areas such as commodity trading, and left Alsace to resettle in Paris, where Robert Louis-Dreyfus was born.

Having graduated with an MBA from Harvard Business School, Louis-Dreyfus worked for a spell in the family business during the mid-seventies before joining IMS, whose president he became in 1984. He was partly credited with boosting the company's value before it was bought by Dunn & Bradstreet in 1988, and was reckoned to have made a not inconsiderable $10 million personally from the deal. When the Saatchis first approached him, Louis-Dreyfus told them immediately that he would take the job only if they agreed to give him enough power to implement his own rescue plans. Charles and Maurice knew they were in a weak position and had no alternative but to agree to his demands.

Charles Scott, the new finance director, had worked with Louis-Dreyfus at IMS since 1982. Born into a Scottish army family, Scott became a qualified accountant, taking the traditional financial director's route to the top, rising from City stockbroker through the finance department of Itel, the distribution and financial services corporation, to IMS. Saatchi's other Charlie was a big man, with large round spectacles that gave him an owlish appearance. An unflamboyant accountant throughout his career, he made a good working partner for Louis-Dreyfus, who had the big financial ideas and needed someone with a love of detail to put them into practice. Like Louis-Dreyfus, he had had no experience of the world of the message merchants until he joined Saatchi & Saatchi in 1990. He didn't mind being called a "bean-counter" by his slick "creatives" and was happy to leave the company's client relationships in the hands of the Saatchi brothers. Unlike Martin

Sorrell, his predecessor, Scott was not the engineer of Saatchi's expansion but rather the manager of its decline. He saw his role, in his own financial-speak, as the disciplined management of core businesses.

Scott remembers having to negotiate an emergency bank loan even before he formally started work at Saatchi & Saatchi PLC. "There were many times in the first fifteen months when I thought, Jesus, how are we going to get out of this mess?" he says. "Believe me, they were tough times." At the outset he presented a financial analysis of the firm's strengths and weaknesses — the kind of detailed review that Louis-Dreyfus preferred to delegate to someone else. Louis-Dreyfus was no dedicated number-cruncher, and not someone given to taking lots of notes, even during important meetings. Although his associates all agree that he is smart and financially adept, when they are asked to describe his talents they usually mention personal rather than professional qualities — a shrewd sense of people and their motives.

Charles Saatchi and Louis-Dreyfus, acquaintances say, struck up an instant rapport, and during the first months of the Frenchman's tenure at Charlotte Street they often played poker together. Before too long, however, they began to move apart. Indeed, after the first year, Charles was barely ever seen at Saatchi's main offices. The company's collapse had changed Charles forever. The man whose single-minded energy and vision had driven Saatchi & Saatchi forward for almost twenty years began to lose interest in the company as soon as he realized that he would have to hand over control. In retrospect, he admits that the physical separation between the company offices in Charlotte Street and Berkeley Square was more than symbolic. "I'm not very good at coping with not running things. Maybe we brought it all on ourselves. Looking back, we had a company that we got into trouble — we went too deep into debt in the eighties and didn't foresee that things would come unglued. We made a terrible mistake and paid the price. We handed over the company to Robert, saying, 'It's yours — you hire and fire who you like, we'll just sit over here. You leave us in peace and you can do whatever you like.' As far as I was concerned, I said I would look after the clients who wanted my interest and Maurice would go on wooing big clients. 'We'll take care of that end and you take care of the business.'"

Louis-Dreyfus claims that he found the company in a far worse condition than Maurice and Charles had originally admitted. "I ought to have done my homework better," he says today. In fact, Saatchi & Saatchi was virtually bankrupt by the beginning of 1990 and Louis-Dreyfus had to move quickly to solve the company's biggest problem, the Euroconvertibles, which were eventually turned into ordinary Saatchi & Saatchi shares. Maurice acceded to the plan. "It was a very painful period," he says. "I wore sackcloth and ashes every day." Nevertheless, he went along with Louis-Dreyfus to the extent that he condescended to withdraw from the management of the company.

Ironically, his eclipse coincided with the emergence of Josephine Hart as a best-selling novelist. In his spare time Maurice threw himself enthusiastically into the role of celebrity consort. "He referred to it as his Denis Thatcher mode," recalls Ed Victor, the literary agent and a close friend. "He took tremendous delight in her success." Yet it is difficult to know how much the low profile owed to his disquiet at the way Louis-Dreyfus was shaking up Saatchi & Saatchi PLC.

The Frenchman's next move was to consolidate his power, removing Roy Warman and Terry Bannister. His grand plan for the company was to focus on the core business of the group — advertising, marketing, media buying, and public relations. Saatchi & Saatchi could no longer hope to be the biggest in the world, but it could still be the best in these fields. The consultancy businesses, it was agreed, would have to go. Louis-Dreyfus loved a deal, but he found he did not enjoy being forced to sell in a falling market. In March, group borrowing peaked at £277 million, but he knew that slowly he was beginning to get the situation under control, and by the end of his first year he had halved the £119 million in earn-out payments owed to managers of the consultancies, successfully averting the need for borrowing a further £30 million.

Nevertheless, rumors of bankruptcy continued to plague the company. In October of that year the magazine industry's trade association, the Periodical Publishers Association, told its members that Saatchi & Saatchi was about to place itself in the hands of the receivers. The PPA quickly put out a full retraction once it realized its mistake, but the company's share price slumped anyway. The whole incident was a painful reminder of Saatchi's delicate position. Louis-Dreyfus plowed on with his cost-cutting plans. Money spent on such items as cars and computers was reduced from £58 million to £20 million, and Louis-Dreyfus himself drove around in a modest Peugeot 205 company car. But it was a struggle to implement all the changes.

"Advertising," he said, "is the most conservative business. I expect if you look at the way agencies were run in the fifties they were run in exactly the same way as they are now. When it comes to producing work they are very creative, forward-thinking places, but when it comes to managing themselves they are still very conservative. I think a recession will force a change in the way things are done."

Soon he turned his attention to the salaries of senior executives, which had continued to rise exponentially during the eighties. When a particular adman, Geoff Seymour, moved to Saatchi & Saatchi in 1982 at a salary rumored to be £100,000, his name entered advertising lexicography as a generic noun. From then on, admen changed jobs for "half a Seymour" or "a Seymour and a bit." But Louis-Dreyfus replaced the large fixed wages of the past with performance-related incentives. "There are still huge fixed salaries in advertising. The trend will have to be towards more normal salaries," he said.

Critics insisted that the Frenchman would eventually be forced to sell off one of the two major advertising networks, Saatchi & Saatchi Worldwide or Backer Spielvogel Bates Worldwide. He told them such a move would be madness in the long term, even if it helped feed Saatchi's hungry bankers over the next few years. Others said the company was considering a move to Docklands, transferring its headquarters and its Charlotte Street agency to Canary Wharf in return for a cash injection and a commitment by the Olympia and York developers to take over its existing property. Some commentators even speculated that the company might consider selling off its share of the Saatchi art collection — estimated to be worth as much as £35 million — though at the same time expressing doubt as to how the art market would react to a sudden glut of paintings. Turning the business around was a slow process, as Paul Bainsfair, managing director of Charlotte Street at the time, pointed out: "The larger accounts have a momentum of their own and require a certain level of service; you can't just crack a whip and demand a greater return for money," he said. "It's a bit like trying to stop an ocean liner in its tracks. What we are trying to do is galvanize ourselves on the new-business front, because it is that sort of organic growth which will become increasingly important." Here Louis-Dreyfus recognized the role of Maurice Saatchi: "Most people would still rather come to lunch with Maurice than with me," he said.

In 1991, in his report to Saatchi & Saatchi shareholders, Louis-Dreyfus attempted to be as upbeat as possible. He told them that the company had managed to sell off ten of the twelve consulting businesses, that the bank debt was down, and that surplus property in the group was being actively marketed to interested companies. He also announced plans for a complex refinancing of the group to ensure its long-term survival, pointing out that with the length and severity of the recession there could be no quick or easy solutions to Saatchi's problems. The refinancing scheme had gone through without a hitch and a £55-million rights issue had provided the group with enough cash to ease the burden of day-to-day costs. For his part, Maurice, who was still chairman of the holding company, told shareholders that the scheme was absolutely crucial for the stable future of the group.

There was palpable relief at Charlotte Street, now under chairman Bill Muirhead. He recognized that the corporate refinancing was more important to the London agency than to any other in Saatchi & Saatchi PLC. Sharing a name with the troubled holding company, combined with all the media attention on Charles and Maurice and their part in the financial chaos, had kept Charlotte Street firmly in the spotlight for a long time. "We'll never know what effect the negative publicity has had on new business," he told *Campaign*. Muirhead started to implement a far-reaching redundancy program for the agency, very overstaffed after the mergers of the eighties. An estimated three hundred jobs were eventually axed out of a total of eight hundred people working for the company at the time. Talk of a possible move to Docklands had done little for morale and the management were struggling to hold on to the most talented copywriters, art directors, and account handlers, who were still in demand even though the job market in advertising as a whole was collapsing.

The industry was in the throes of a deep recession. According to the Institute of Practitioners in Advertising, the number of people in the industry dropped from a 1989 high of 15,400 to 11,000 by 1993. The days of admen in red suspenders and Porsches were fast disappearing, as were the lavish agency parties of the eighties. Saatchi & Saatchi had been one of the last of the great party-throwers. For a celebrated bash at Alexandra Palace in 1989, the year before the brothers handed over control to Louis-Dreyfus, both sides of Charlotte Street had been re-created in north London. Now the agency was forced to match the more sober mood of the times, making use, on occasion, of the Charlotte Street car park for its parties. Ostentation, yuppies, power dressing, and nouvelle cuisine were all out in the advertising industry of the nineties. In 1984 *Campaign* had reported that drug abuse was rampant in the advertising industry, estimating that the going rate for a gram of cocaine was around £60. It was another sign of the times. The problem was particularly bad in commercials production, where drugs had become standard currency. By 1993, the same magazine was telling its readers that the widespread use of drugs was a thing of the past.

Maurice was coming under increasing pressure to play a more active role in attracting big new clients. "This image of

Maurice as a client schmoozer is a relatively new thing," says one former Saatchi insider. "When things were going well, it seemed like he never did any work at all, while Charles was always the completely dominant figure. It's only two or three years ago that he started reinventing himself as a client man, once the pressure was on. You have to remember that all these people are revisionists, operating to their own private agenda. They will say whatever suits their purpose at the time."

The relationship between Louis-Dreyfus and Charles Saatchi cooled even further when the Frenchman tried to press the reclusive brother into service. Insiders complained that Charles spent too much time on his art collection and not enough on copywriting, an activity that, in reality, he had more or less abandoned years before as he concentrated on masterminding the group's expansion. But Louis-Dreyfus also recognized that Charles, with an annual salary of £625,000, would be a very expensive disposal. In fact, both brothers had five-year contracts with the company, and although Maurice was occasionally to be spotted at the lavish lunches he hosted for senior industrialists, where new business prospects could mix freely with glamorous celebrities, Charles was rarely seen in public. There was growing pressure for Charles to step down and take on some kind of face-saving role as a consultant or a nonexecutive director, with his salary slashed and the Saatchi entourage in Berkeley Square drastically reduced. By now the brothers were the only people left at the company's opulent "headquarters." The rest of the holding company had moved into more modest offices behind Charlotte Street, as part of the cost-cutting program. At a meeting in January 1991, shareholders called for the brothers to take a cut in salary. One even asked Maurice to cut his annual remuneration to £100,000, demanding that he also offer a rebate to the company from his previous year's pay packet as a way of reflecting its poor performance. The company secretary replied that Maurice was taking only half his salary that year, after waiving 30 percent of it the previous year. To alleviate more of the pressure, Charles and Maurice announced they would be investing £600,000 in new shares in the company, while two hundred other managers, including Louis-Dreyfus, said they would be subscribing to another £5 million worth of shares.

By September 1991 the *Guardian* was commenting that "The latest bulletin from the sickbed of Saatchi & Saatchi shows the patient had been moved from intensive care and is now on the recovery ward. The transfusion of this spring's recapitalization has stabilized its financial position, but the patient remains weak. Convalescence would be aided by a less debilitating climate, but that is only likely to improve with time. The doctor in charge, Robert Louis-Dreyfus, says, barring a deterioration in the climate, no further surgery will be required. But he estimates it will be three years before the patient is restored to full health and able to pay a dividend again."

Yet Saatchi & Saatchi was already returning to a more stable position. The cost cutting and debt reduction were gradually bringing the company back from the brink of collapse.

Then, in April 1993, Louis-Dreyfus was approached by French financiers to help Crédit Lyonnais, the troubled French state bank, sort out one of its most troubled investments, the ailing German sportswear firm Adidas. Louis-Dreyfus had spent more than three years at Saatchi & Saatchi, working hard to stop the banks from calling in the receivers, but now he signaled he had

had enough. He was replaced by his lieutenant Charles Scott, although he did maintain a position on the board. When he finally cut his ties with the agency, he left behind a loss of some £600 million, which had mostly been the result of writing off the losses of previous years, but the underlying position of the company was much improved. According to Michael Bungey, chief executive of Bates Worldwide, Maurice was glad to see the last of the Frenchman. "There once was a train set," he explains. "It went off the tracks, so Charlie Scott and Robert Louis-Dreyfus were brought in to fix it. Many of us said, 'Watch out — as soon as the train's mended, the brothers will want it back.' And that's exactly what happened." Perhaps Maurice felt he had been tricked. He had brought in Louis-Dreyfus, who was debonair, rich, unconventional, but now he had been left with Scott, a gray man in a suit, a bean-counter. In any case, as a parting gesture, Louis-Dreyfus persuaded the brothers to join him in a private deal, an insignificant purchase of some Adidas stock.

Scott immediately initiated a review of the group's strategy and in the spring of 1993 he returned to the stock market for more money, asking shareholders to support a £73-million rights issue. Saatchi's American interests were becoming a particular area of concern to Scott. During the black time of the advertising recession in the late 1980s and early 1990s, Saatchi & Saatchi's financial performance in the U.S. was distinctly lackluster. The Saatchis recognized that the American ad market was going to be critical to the recovery of the whole group, representing as it did 40 percent of the world's ad revenues. However, growth continued to prove elusive, long after the situation had begun to improve in the U.K. Saatchi stocks had become one of the worst performing of the period, as the U.S. market seemed to completely lose faith in the company, one investor even referring to it as "the company that just about everyone on Wall Street loves to hate." Client losses such as Chrysler-Jeep with $25 million and Helene Curtis hair products with $80 million continued to hit the beleaguered U.S. agencies in the early 1990s.

In 1993, growth in total U.S. advertising revenue was estimated at 3.8 percent, making it one of the worst-performing years since 1944. And in that year Saatchi did worse than most, slipping in the rankings from fourth place the previous year to seventh. While Saatchi & Saatchi could still list among its clients some of the continent's biggest advertisers, including General Mills and Hewlett Packard, the group was struggling to win new business and produce interesting creative work, and it was clear that its staff was both demoralized and unmotivated.

Back in London, plans were hatched to try to reverse the fortunes of the U.S. Saatchi agencies. The company had three agency organizations in the U.S., run separately to cope with client conflict. Significant changes were made in each. "I have taken the best people I have around the world and put them in America, because America is so important," Charles Scott told the press in 1994. "In our business, if you underperform in America, it doesn't matter how well you do in smaller markets."

At Bates Worldwide a new management team was hired, including as chief executive Michael Bungey, the man who had effectively been running the company since the beginning of 1993. And it was at Bates that recovery first started to show its face. The client list had some impressive names, firms such as Mars, Wendy's, and Heinz, but the company still had an underdog feel to it. Under the leadership of Bungey the situation began to change. By 1994, when Ogilvy & Mather was awarded IBM advertising around the

111

world and thereby forced to resign its relationship with IBM rival Compaq, it was Bates that picked up the $50-million-a-year Compaq account. Even more surprising, one of Bates's main accounts before the agency reorganization in 1986, the drug company Warner Lambert, which had moved its advertising budget elsewhere immediately after the Saatchi acquisition, named Bates as its main agency in 1994, giving it an account worth some $70 million a year. When Miller gave Bates its $40-million Lite Ice account in the same year, there was no denying that recovery, for Bates at least, was well under way.

At the smaller Minneapolis-based Campbell Mithun Esty, Saatchi's third network, the company was still reeling from the loss of the Chrysler account, but a new management team, including a new chief operating officer and a new financial officer, had been installed in the hope of turning around the agency's fortunes. The agency had been merged with one of Saatchi's U.K. agencies, KHBB, in 1992 to form an operation renamed CME.KHBB, with the idea that it might one day form the basis of a third international advertising network.

At the end of 1993, Charles Scott presented his strategy review to the company's board. He had concluded that the Saatchi group's present structure gave the company the best chance of building on the beginnings of the recovery started under his predecessor, Louis-Dreyfus. The board readily accepted his recommendations. At the same time Charles Saatchi finally agreed to resign from the board — after twenty-three years of not attending a single board meeting. "Charles didn't like the way the company was going or the people who were now running it and the way they were treating Maurice," says one of his friends. "He had a nice life and he said he just didn't need the grief anymore. When

112

he heard that the board was jubilant when Maurice told them of his decision, he didn't know whether to be hurt or pleased." Scott told shareholders in the annual report that 1993 had been a "challenging year" for the company. The outlook for 1994 he described as "demanding." In other words, the problems at Saatchi & Saatchi PLC were not yet over.

seven FIGHT STARTER

*O*NE REASON WHY the story of David Herro's career is of interest to others besides the shareholders in various multinational companies is that David Herro is not all that unusual. Yet this thirty-three-year-old American wunderkind, who by the end of 1993 held a 10 percent stake in Saatchi & Saatchi, had a lot in common with Maurice Saatchi. Although they had never met, both men were ambitious and successful at a young age and both enjoyed big cars and expensive lifestyles. Like the Saatchi brothers, Herro was an outsider. He had come to Chicago from the town of Fond du Lac in Wisconsin, a farming and industrial community not far from Milwaukee. But while Maurice, the proud owner of various Bentleys, enjoyed spending time at his Sussex mansion in the company of Josephine Hart and a host of celebrities, Herro, tall and athletic-looking, with dark curly hair, lived a solitary existence, his favorite pastime working out at the gym near his deluxe apartment in Chicago's Gold Coast district.

At his local Catholic high school, Herro was known as a tough kid. Some of his friends called him FS, pronounced Fess after Fess Parker, the actor who played Davy Crockett in the sixties television series. Others, however, claim that the nickname also stood for Fight Starter. "He was always acting like a scholarly little schoolboy and had the nuns wrapped around his little finger," says a boyhood friend. "But when he thought something was wrong, he was a wild man."

Herro's interest in the stock market began when he was twelve, and after graduating with a master's in economics from the University of Wisconsin, he landed his first job as a share analyst at the age of twenty-six. He went on from there to launch an international fund for the Principal Financial Group, in Des Moines, and three years later he joined the State of Wisconsin Investment Board, in charge of investing a $400-million public employee investment fund in international financial markets. Then in 1992 the Chicago-based investment company Harris Associates, impressed by his track record, offered him the chance to start up his own fund, Oakmark International. He was so confident of success, he told the *Wall Street Journal,* that he spent only $150 on advertising to launch the fund. During Oakmark's first year its earnings were flat, but in 1993 they were up by 55 percent, and new money came flooding in. He had made Oakmark into one of the best-performing diversified international funds in the country.

Herro had been interested in Saatchi & Saatchi for a considerable time. He thought the company looked undervalued, and yet he had never bought any shares in it because he felt uneasy about the Saatchi brothers' financial management. As soon as they handed over control of the company to Louis-Dreyfus and Scott, the American whiz kid started to buy Saatchi & Saatchi shares enthusiastically. He admired Louis-Dreyfus and Scott, and believed that they could restore the company to financial health — to such an extent that, by the time Louis-Dreyfus left the company, Herro's fund was the company's largest shareholder, owning 9.98 percent of the stock. Moreover, the State of Wisconsin Investment Board, with which Herro still had strong ties, held another 8 percent.

In his eagerness for short-term advantage, Herro invariably stepped on other people's toes. By 1994 he was beginning to pay the price. Perhaps it was just a question of his luck running out. In the first quarter of the year Oakmark was outperformed by many of its rivals for the first time in the two years since it had been established. Even some of the fund's investors started calling Herro's office for an explanation, and it is clear from his words in that year's annual report that he was under pressure. "I am pleased to say that during this difficult period most shareholders remained very patient, despite gyrations of the market and the effect on the fund," he wrote. The reputation for stock-picking prudence that Herro had struggled to acquire began to dissipate.

Herro himself was a much less patient and supportive shareholder than Oakmark's uneasy investors. Saatchi & Saatchi was just one of more than fifty companies in which the fund had a stake, but it was also one of the most famous names. His concerns about the advertising agency had been triggered at the beginning of the year by a number of reports in the London press about a dispute between one of the founders, Maurice Saatchi, and the new chief executive, Charles Scott. The two men had been publicly falling out over the best way to rescue the company from its financial difficulties. "It's a double whammy," Maurice had told the *Sunday Times,* in a direct attack on Scott's ability to manage the agency. "We've lost market share, we've lost good people, and we've spent £37 million on redundancies for nothing. Staff costs are as high as ever." Scott retaliated in the same article with the complaint that the company was not winning enough new business, officially Maurice's area of responsibility. "In advertising, your assets are your people, and there have to be salary rises. We can't cut costs to prosperity. You get there by winning new business," he said.

The newspaper had reported a meeting between Charles Scott and Tim Jackson, Saatchi's head of investor relations, which it said had taken place six months before. It was a routine meeting, the kind of rehearsal many chief executives go through before facing questions from City analysts. During the meeting Maurice Saatchi had appeared at the door and Scott invited him to join them. They were discussing staff costs and, according to the report, Scott seemed unable to explain why they were higher now than before the redundancy program. "For it to have happened at all [Maurice] reasoned was bad enough," wrote the *Sunday Times,* "but for Scott, the self-styled 'bean-counter,' not to have noticed was even worse. In any case, the brothers were already furious with Louis-Dreyfus for landing them with Scott. 'They complained they had hired a charismatic character and he had left them with a bean-counter,' said a Saatchi friend. 'They felt they had a finance director as a chief executive, and they couldn't see how an advertising company could be run by a finance director who knew nothing about the business.' "

In fact, Scott was beginning to get the astronomical staff costs under control. Big pay raises had been a particular problem in 1990 and 1991, when salaries had been raised just before the advertising recession, and the real difficulty now was the lack of new business. But the press war continued unabated, while other unsettling rumors began to appear. The *Observer* reported that the brothers were plotting a £200-million management buyout of Saatchi & Saatchi Advertising. Emily Bell, the newspaper's advertising correspondent, wrote: "Considering the turmoil Saatchi has endured in the last five years, it is unthinkable that it may be on the brink of another management crisis."

Having spent years in his "cupboard" paying for the sins of the past, Maurice began to feel it was time to rejoin the action. He took the initiative and brought in a distinguished new member of the board. At the beginning of 1994 Sir Peter Walters, a former head of BP and Midland Bank, came on the board as a nonexecutive director. According to Maurice, Walters took the view that Charles Scott was indeed more like a finance director than a chief executive, and urged Maurice to be "more assertive" as chairman. "Maurice took what I said as a personal blessing to turn on Charlie Scott," says Walters.

Maurice looked for his chance. In February 1994, having become fed up with the poor performance of Saatchi & Saatchi Advertising in America, Scott fired its chief executive, Bob Kennedy. Unfortunately for Scott, Kennedy's contract meant that sacking him cost the company $6 million. Here was the opportunity Maurice had been looking for. Immediately he began an undercover attack on Scott in the press, blaming his ineptitude for the fact that the company was still in such trouble despite an economic recovery in Britain and the U.S. Both Maurice and Scott hired public relations men in the early spring of 1994 to spin their side of the story to the newspapers. "The whole world knows that Maurice tried to get me fired," says Scott. Maurice consulted David Burnside, a former British Airways employee, who had recently started his own public relations business. "The time is approaching for Maurice Saatchi, who has played a detached role as chairman, to become more actively involved in direct strategy," wrote the *Evening Standard*. Other newspapers echoed this view; it was as if they had completely forgotten how Maurice and his brother Charles had been responsible for bringing the company to the brink of bankruptcy in the first place.

In the roadshow to promote his fight back, Maurice was uncharacteristically voluble about his vision for the future of the company, although perhaps he was unwise to invest so lavishly in professional expertise. Burnside later filed a $50,000 bill to Saatchi & Saatchi through Bill Muirhead, who by then had been appointed the head of the company's U.S. operation. "It was broken down into three items," says a senior Saatchi & Saatchi executive who has seen the invoice, "including work for the chairman's office." In many ways, of course, the use of a press agent was only to be expected. As a rule, Maurice prefers not to meet the press face to face, and he seldom gives interviews. "Maurice doesn't like his fingerprints on things," Tim Bell observes. In 1995, when asked by a *Vanity Fair* reporter if Burnside had indeed been working for him in placing critical stories, Maurice Saatchi just replied, "Um, there was a press war."

Sitting in his fifth-floor offices at Two LaSalle Street in Chicago, David Herro was worried by the attacks on Charles Scott in the press. "Our policy was to buy into good companies when they are in trouble, and in the case of Saatchi & Saatchi its share price had gone through the floor," says Herro. "We bought into the new management of Robert Louis-Dreyfus and Charles Scott. The Saatchis had nearly ruined the company and no one would have put up the refinancing money without the new management. When I went to Harris Associates things were looking much better for Saatchi, although there were still problems with revenue growth, so we invested. Then, from our point of view, we could see someone trying to get rid of the very management —

that is, Charles Scott — in which we had invested our money, and we couldn't allow that to happen. I have to be responsible to my shareholders for the performance of my fund, after all."

So Herro decided to take the rather unusual step, in U.K. terms, of writing directly to the chairman, Maurice Saatchi, to express his dismay. He emphasized how damaging the negative publicity could be to a company like Saatchi & Saatchi in what he described as the "image-related business." He wrote, "The most distressing aspect of this, however, is the possibility that the source of this publicity has been from the Saatchi board members," in a direct hint that he suspected Maurice himself of initiating the press war. Maurice sent Herro a swift reply, agreeing that indeed the bad publicity was not good for the company, though unable to resist adding an indirect attack on Scott. "It is painful to watch our rivals moving ahead while we still remain somewhat in the doldrums," he wrote.

In spite of Herro's warning, the war of attrition between the chairman and the chief executive continued. A month after his first letter, Herro wrote again. This time he claimed to have discussed his concerns with other shareholders, representing some 30 percent of the company's shares. His demand was blunt: "Specifically, the Company needs a chairman who will be more complementary to and compatible with the chief executive, Charles Scott." He added: "Through my investigation and observation, it is clear that the current chairman, Maurice Saatchi, does not fill this need. Realizing there are risks to a change of this nature, it should be recognized that there are greater long-term risks if this situation is not dealt with in a swift and certain manner." Herro's letter was followed by one from John Nelson, an investment director at the State of Wisconsin Investment Board. "I believe," he wrote, "that whosoever serves as chairman of the Company should be fully committed to aiding Charles Scott in generating new business, lowering the cost structure, and guiding the company to long-term success. If this requires replacing the current chairman, Mr. Saatchi, then it should be done."

David Herro was under pressure from his own shareholders and he was afraid. If the Saatchi brothers were trying to raise enough money to buy back Saatchi & Saatchi Advertising, it was difficult to see how they could also be protecting his interests as a shareholder. He could not help reminding himself that the brothers' own misjudgments had nearly destroyed the company at the end of the previous decade. He wanted to be sure that Maurice really could, as he promised, open the door to big new business opportunities. Maurice Saatchi enjoyed a huge income, officially £625,000, although Herro knew he was actually taking only half of his entitlement. He was also on a rolling five-year contract. Herro thought Maurice was making a lot of money out of Saatchi & Saatchi and he wanted to find out exactly how many hours a day this highly paid executive spent earning his big salary, how often he was actually in the office.

David Herro came from an American tradition of shareholder activism. While British institutional investors frequently do not exercise their rights to appoint and sack directors, American shareholders have become increasingly involved in the running of the companies in which they have a stake. And U.K. companies are aware, as these U.S. companies start to increase their investments overseas, that they are also starting to export their policy of shareholder activism. In America the forced removal of chairmen has lately become a part of corporate fashion — the public use of shareholder power to unseat unsatisfactory management almost commonplace — and David Herro's previous employer, the State of Wisconsin, is among the most active of American institutional investors. Each year a number of these, including the State of Wisconsin, publish a list of the companies they intend to upbraid on the grounds that they are underperforming. Invariably, this exercise in transparency leads to public showdowns.

In this context, David Herro thought he was acting in a perfectly legitimate manner by asking Saatchi & Saatchi difficult questions about the behavior of its senior directors. He simply wanted to get to the bottom of the Saatchi problems. "David is a man of strong convictions," says one of his friends. "It is his way or no way. He's very intense. Sometimes he won't even listen to you long enough for you to make a point." He goes on, "There's a pretty good chance he's right about Saatchi. He's not an advertising guy, but he knows where to spot problems and he really will have looked over the numbers thousands and thousands of times. He lives and breathes numbers. They are his passion."

At the end of March, David Herro went to London for a private lunch with Maurice Saatchi in the Berkeley Square offices, which the Saatchi brothers had still not vacated. "Success breeds success," argued Maurice, "and clients like their agencies to be housed in offices which make them look successful and confident. This is a fashion business," he said, "and it is very important to have the right image." So at a time when hundreds of people were being fired from the Saatchi group and costs were being cut to the bone, the company continued to lay out £1 million a year for Berkeley Square, a sum that also provided for the Saatchi brothers' personal entourage, including two tea ladies, a receptionist, two personal assistants, an accountant, and various secretaries.

This was the first time Maurice Saatchi and David Herro had

met face to face. Maurice claims to remember very little about the occasion. Herro, however, remembers that the food was excellent and at the end of the meal there were expensive cigars. As they adjourned for coffee he noticed someone nervously peering around the open door of the room, trying to catch snatches of the conversation. But the minute Herro caught the eye of the mysterious stranger, he quickly disappeared. Herro asked Maurice who this eavesdropper could be, but Maurice was evasive and simply changed the subject. Only later did Herro discover that, as well as meeting Maurice that day, he had caught his first glimpse of the more reclusive Saatchi brother, Charles.

After the lunch, Herro made no secret of the fact that he disliked Maurice, reportedly describing him as a "toffee-nosed Brit."

"I'll never forget," says an Oakmark source, "at the end of lunch Maurice takes out this big box of cigars, lights one up, looks out over the most expensive real estate in London. He says, 'What are we going to do about all these expenses?' I mean, knock, knock. Is there anybody home? What a way to run a company!" But what most vexed Herro was the way Maurice responded when he suggested that, as chairman, Maurice might indicate his confidence in the future of the company by investing in a few more shares himself. Maurice claims that he said he would consider it, but according to Herro, Maurice replied that investing in more Saatchi stock would simply be too risky. Not surprisingly, perhaps, the chairman's lack of confidence in his own company did not go down very well with his main shareholder.

"Maurice is a slightly childlike figure sometimes," one of his close associates says. "He's quite incredibly charming and beguiling, but he just doesn't see that some things are an issue. I would personally feel embarrassed to drive around in a Bentley — I just would. There's something slightly antisocial about it — especially if my employees didn't have a pay rise for three years and I'm having to face them every day and they've all had their company cars taken away. But the funny thing was that the employees wanted him to have a Bentley. The employees wanted him to be in a castle with a wife who writes fantastic books, because that says he's successful. When I talked about these things with Maurice — which I did a lot — he would smile at me and say, 'But that's me, that's how I am.' He was exactly like that when he was twenty-one. Nothing's changed. I don't know why anybody is surprised."

The big cars and extravagant spending did offend David Herro, but not as much as the press war Maurice waged against Charles Scott. "I started thinking, hmm — is this how a chairman of a company should react when someone is trying to help the company?" Herro says. "Should the chairman try to get his CEO fired in an overt public relations battle that is harming the reputation of a company that is supposed to be involved in imagery?"

The day after Herro's lunch with Maurice Saatchi, the company's nonexecutive directors met prior to a full board meeting to try and resolve the dispute between the chairman and the chief executive. While Scott had the support of the company's key shareholders, it was understood that Maurice had important links with some of the group's biggest clients, including Mars and British Airways. It was left to Jeremy Sinclair to provide a brief summary of the board's predicament.

It was a delicate task, not least because Sinclair had been with the brothers for a great number of years and was fiercely, profoundly loyal to them. He knew who were their friends and who their enemies. More important, he knew the members of the board very well. He had carefully studied each of them for years; he had slowly turned their characters over in his mind, knowing their idiosyncrasies and weaknesses. He had been privy to their quarrels — the quarrels by which life at Saatchi & Saatchi PLC was defined and invigorated — and he had chosen sides, had discriminated and judged. In making his judgments and discriminations, however, he had picked up certain habits of mind from the brothers, together with a certain tone, a tone that he deployed in summarizing the board's dilemma on this particular occasion. "Who's the best door opener in the business?" he asked. "Maurice Saatchi. And who's the best at handling the company's finances? Charles Scott. So you've got to start from a completely different premise. You've got to start from the premise that we need both of them."

Scott and Maurice eventually, under pressure from the other directors, agreed to a truce, and as part of the peace deal the board announced it was planning to hire a senior advertising and marketing executive "to guide and direct the revenue and development of Saatchi." David Herro was intrigued by this new turn of events. He remembered being told quite specifically that it was Maurice's job to bring in new clients. If he really was the best new-business man in the industry, why was the company looking for this new recruit? he wanted to know. On April 5 he wrote again, this time to Sir Peter Walters, asking that the board "remain extremely diligent in monitoring this situation and consider the chairman's past record when determining compensation and expense budgets." A week later Herro placed a call to Saatchi's head of investor relations in London to ask about the procedure required to put a special resolution to shareholders. The implication was clear. He was considering calling an extraordinary general meeting to attempt to oust Maurice Saatchi from the company. Then suddenly Herro remembered that Maurice Saatchi was actually up for reelection at the company's annual general meeting in the summer. If the board would not remove him before, he would vote against Maurice publicly at the AGM. There would be no need for an EGM after all.

The board directors were now getting very nervous. They knew that the public sacking of one of the company's two founders by an institutional shareholder from America would be a public relations disaster, especially for an advertising group still performing less well than its competitors. Jeremy Sinclair worked hard to persuade the board that they should make one last attempt to talk Herro out of his terrible plan. He volunteered to fly to Herro's offices in Chicago, and Charles Scott and Clive Gibson agreed to go with him.

Back in Chicago, David Herro had been doing some homework, reading the Cadbury Report on Corporate Governance, published in the U.K. at the end of 1992. Chaired by Sir Adrian Cadbury, former chairman of the chocolate company, the Cadbury Committee had aimed to spread the boardroom practices of the best-run companies to those that were less well managed. The report specified that it was the chairman's job to ensure the company was run along the lines of "good corporate governance." That was enough for David Herro, who still believed Maurice had initiated the press campaign against Charles Scott and in so doing had helped to upset the company's prospects of recovery, at least in the short term. According to Cadbury, Maurice should have been acting in the best interests of shareholders, not waging his own private war against the chief executive. Maurice had to be made to realize, thought Herro, that Saatchi & Saatchi no longer belonged to him and his brother. They had given up their controlling interest long ago to fund their doomed acquisition program and now they could be held to account for their actions by the new owners, the institutional shareholders, including himself.

The meeting in Chicago with the Saatchi & Saatchi directors lasted for almost three hours. Herro was determined to get his own way. He felt that Maurice had behaved badly and he did not trust him. If the board would not act against Maurice, he said, he was prepared to do so himself. Jeremy Sinclair argued that Saatchi's clients respected Maurice, and told Herro how committed the chairman really was to getting back on the new-business trail. He was determined, said Sinclair, to work hard to turn the company around. Herro and John Nelson, who was on the phone from the State of Wisconsin Investment Board's offices, brought up their concerns about Maurice's five-year rolling contract and overgenerous salary. They said they were in favor of shorter fixed contracts that gave managers more of an incentive to work hard. Sinclair thought they could reach a deal. Maurice, he was sure, would be prepared to change his contract and to guarantee that, as he had always done, he would put the interests of shareholders above everything else. Herro and Nelson proposed a fixed three-year contract for Maurice with a basic salary of £200,000 and a series of bonuses that would be tied to the fortunes of Saatchi & Saatchi's share price.

In the end Maurice said yes, he would accept a pay cut, would get more involved in the business — and would even think about changing the name of the holding company from Saatchi & Saatchi PLC to avoid confusion with Saatchi & Saatchi Advertising. The company's name had been causing controversy in the group for some time. Many of the senior executives felt that the close association between the holding company and one of its advertising networks relegated the other divisions to the status of second-class citizens. Whenever Maurice succeeded in attracting a big new client, it was always billed as a triumph for Saatchi & Saatchi, leaving the other divisions demoralized by the fact that they never seemed to get a mention. But Maurice had always been adamant that he would never work for a company that didn't call itself Saatchi & Saatchi. "I didn't see much merit in taking down the most famous name in advertising," he remembers. The only attractive part of Maurice's new contract with the company was a stock-option plan that would reward him with options worth up to £5 million. He would be able to exercise them, it said, between three and ten years after the agreement was signed.

In spite of his various concessions, Maurice remained unconvinced that David Herro would be satisfied. He was aware that before this new agreement it would have been very expensive for the company to get rid of him. Now, with a three-year contract and a reduced salary of just £200,000, his removal would be much cheaper. According to Maurice, his brother warned him that the new contract was merely storing up trouble for the future. He recalls, "Charles, who has a very blunt view of these things, told me, 'You're a fool. All you're doing is agreeing to your cheaper sacking in six months' time.' He was right. I did it under pressure from Herro personally. I was very unhappy, but I did it." Undoubtedly Maurice realized that he could have left the company with a big payoff instead of acceding to the new terms of employment. The real problem, according to Charles, was a sentimental attachment. The beleaguered chairman was unable even to contemplate leaving the company he had founded. "I said to Maurice," Charles remembers, "'At the most, even though you're only drawing half your salary, you have a five-year contract. You've got too many enemies on the board who want you out. If you give up that contract, this chap Herro can't be trusted, and he'll come back and get you and then you'll have nothing.' Maurice isn't terribly motivated by money. He's motivated by success and by doing something well. I always thought, if they left him alone to do what he wanted to do, which is look after the clients, he would've paid them £20,000 or whatever it would take for the job. He would have paid them to have the job — that's how much he loved it — so you can imagine the pain he went through when all this went on. It was awful."

In fact, long opposed to what he regarded as a sellout, Maurice fought hard to get the best terms possible in his new contract with the company. He knew he could rely on support from valuable clients such as Sir Colin Marshall, chairman of British Airways, who wrote to Sir Peter Walters expressing his concern about the threat to Maurice's position. The airline had been working with Saatchi & Saatchi for many years, he said, and "during all of this time, Maurice Saatchi has been the driving force and key linchpin behind the relationship, to the extent that our relatively new partner, Qantas Airways, is giving serious consideration, on our recommendation, to placing its worldwide account with Saatchi. In the event that Maurice should no longer be in a position to direct our advertising strategy we would have to consider our own position as well as the foregoing recommendation. To be more specific I believe that it is essential to have a real advertising 'pro' at the head of the agency to better reassure the Company's long-standing clients." A second precious Saatchi & Saatchi client also wrote to the company, this time via Maurice himself. Forrest Mars said that his working relationship with Maurice was crucial to the service they had from the agency. If he were to go, Mars warned, they "might and probably would have to transfer our business to your competitors." The Mars account was worth £30 million to Saatchi & Saatchi. Five days later, Sinclair wrote to Herro to confirm that Maurice had agreed to his new terms and conditions.

Maurice delayed finally signing his new contract right up to the last possible minute, in the hope of securing more favorable terms. He was particularly anxious about his share options and he wanted the board to guarantee them, something that was outside the board's power to do. In the end he signed and the annual general meeting in June went without a hitch, with Maurice reelected as chairman. At last everyone seemed happy, or relatively happy. Even David Herro seemed content. That summer he sent Jeremy Sinclair a handwritten note that read: "Congratulations on all of the recent Saatchi events! I do feel that the changes that were recently made will add to the momentum. Thanks again for your help and dedication."

eight   SAATCHI ISN'T WORKING

*D*AVID HERRO KEPT HIS EYE on Maurice Saatchi's every move during the weeks and months that followed the annual general meeting. As far as he and his fellow fund managers were concerned, Maurice had been lucky to survive the threat to sack him earlier in the year, and he was still in a delicate position. Herro considered Maurice on parole. In his view, the chairman of a public company was only there to serve the interests of the shareholders, and he expected Maurice to tread very carefully from now on. Herro was prepared to give his erring chairman one more chance, despite the attempts of some Saatchi & Saatchi board members to poison his view of the flamboyant adman, among them the non-executive director and father of Maurice's cherished globalization theories Theodore Levitt, who over the years had lost respect for his Saatchi protégé.

Herro remained particularly concerned about Maurice's continuing reluctance to change the holding company's name. The problem had been highlighted when the Bates agency's new Compaq computer account had been mistakenly reported as a Saatchi & Saatchi win. Saatchi & Saatchi Advertising already worked for

Compaq's rival Hewlett Packard, and that company was not amused by the confusion. But Maurice had other things on his mind. Despite all the trouble with David Herro earlier in the year, he was still complaining about Charles Scott and the problem of the company's rising costs. He wanted to carry out a new strategy review of the group's future. The board, anxious to keep the chairman happy after the turmoil of the previous six months, eventually gave in to his demands and on Sir Peter Walters's recommendation they employed an independent consultant, Suzanna Taverne, to carry out the work.

Taverne quickly determined the group had only three basic options: it could merge all its companies, saving on costs but potentially driving away many of its clients through conflicts of interest; it could demerge one or more of its divisions — a choice favored by Maurice, who would have liked to disband the holding company altogether and put himself back at the helm of Saatchi & Saatchi Advertising as an independent operation; or it could retain its current structure. Taverne's conclusions were, first, that the company should retain its current shape, as neither merger nor demerger were realistic options, and second, that the holding company should change its name to distinguish itself more clearly from Saatchi & Saatchi Advertising. Maurice was disappointed at the findings, and furious that Taverne had come out in favor of a name change. He insisted that she not mention the name issue at all in her formal report to the board.

Taverne's report was not the only one presented to the board at a special two-day meeting in October. Over the summer, management consultants Arthur Anderson had been asked to carry out a review of company pensions and remunerations. They had also been asked to draw up the details of Maurice's share-option plan, the one discussed in principle with David Herro earlier in the year. Maurice insisted that if the plan said he could exercise all his share options in between three and ten years, he could, if he chose, exercise the whole lot after just three years. The size of the options, known in fact as superoptions because they represented eight rather than the more usual four times his salary, had been calculated on the basis of his old salary of £625,000 a year, not his new one of £200,000.

When the details of Maurice's scheme were made known to shareholders, there was an outcry. Compared to the rewards for other senior managers in the company, Maurice Saatchi's package looked excessive. On November 17, David Herro resurfaced. He told the board in yet another letter that he was still concerned about the lack of action on the issue of the name change, and that he was offended by Maurice's share-option scheme. He said he thought it was just too generous. "It appears that this Super Option Scheme was not formed in a fair and objective manner," his letter went on. "The various shareholders I have spoken with were not only outraged by the gross amount of the plan, but by the very inequalities of the plan itself. The plan seems to also be very destabilizing to the employees of the operating companies, for they see it as another example of extravagance at the holding company level." Herro also brought up the issue of the company's name, urging the board to "once again re-examine the issue of the holding company management, as well as the holding company name," in a thinly disguised threat to Maurice's position.

Jeremy Sinclair was horrified. As far as he was concerned Herro had personally agreed to the share-option proposal back in May, but now it seemed that he was going back on his word. The man had no integrity, he thought, and it seemed to him that the group was in the grip of someone who could not be trusted. The board was shaken by the shareholders' reaction too. Once again the chairman was under pressure, only this time it was from more than just a couple of maverick American fund holders. British investors had also protested at the proposal, which they said was outside U.K. institutional guidelines. David Herro himself regretted ever agreeing to the outline plan in the first place, although he insisted he had not been aware at the time that it breached U.K. guidelines. He was forced to admit to himself that he had made a bad decision. Herro was aware that some of the company's biggest clients were particularly close to Maurice and it would still be dangerous to sack him, but he was no longer interested in Maurice Saatchi as an asset to the company. The chairman was putting his own interests above those of the company, and David Herro as a major shareholder would not be so easily placated a second time.

Maurice was also facing a shift in public opinion on the issue of corporate pay. The debate about boardroom salary increases had been gaining more press coverage and there were calls over the summer for a halt to the kind of "flexible" schemes that rewarded directors handsomely even when their companies were doing badly. The whole tone of the debate was set by Sir Ian Vallance, the seventy-hour-a-week chairman of British Telecom who, when questioned about the size of his salary and benefits, claimed he worked so hard for them that he might find the job of a junior doctor "relaxing" in comparison. None of this was the fault of Maurice Saatchi, but he was foolish to ignore it as he continued to push for what he insisted had been previously agreed. Word began to travel through the ranks of Saatchi & Saatchi that Maurice was under threat again.

Bill Muirhead, now stationed in New York, was appalled at the efforts against Maurice at this point, when it seemed that the company was making something of a new start. Fresh from running Saatchi & Saatchi's successful Charlotte Street flagship agency in London, Muirhead had arrived in New York in the spring of 1994, his mission, to sort out the mess at Saatchi's U.S. headquarters on Hudson Street. He brought with him Alan Bishop from the London office as chief operating officer. Bishop was blunt about the U.S. company's problems. "The management team just didn't have the support of the agency," he said later.

"It was a bit like British Airways had been when we had first started working for them," said Muirhead. "There was one name on the door, but inside it was still several different airlines." The agency had been founded by the merger of two existing agencies in 1987, Dancer Fitzgerald Sample and Saatchi & Saatchi Compton, which together had formed Saatchi & Saatchi Worldwide, with its main North American subsidiary in New York christened Saatchi & Saatchi DFS Compton. Seven years later, Muirhead found that the agency was still operating as two separate entities under the same roof — not an effective way to run a company, he concluded. Although the New York agency had only lost one account in the previous three years, clients like Burger King and parts of Sara Lee were on the brink of jumping ship as he arrived. More conspicuously, the agency had failed to win any new clients during that time and there had been several painful rounds of staff reductions. "The picture was depressingly clear," he said. "The company had not won any new business, was not doing any interesting work, and most of the staff were deeply unhappy."

Muirhead acted quickly and decisively, sacking Harvey Hoffenberg, the creative director and chairman, and Richard Pounder, the vice chairman, and replacing them with Michael Jeary, from the San Francisco agency, and Stanley Becker, who came in to sort out the creative department. Becker had been the man in charge of the successful Toyota account in California.

Less visibly, Muirhead then set to work reorganizing the entire company along the lines of Charlotte Street. Out went the old-fashioned pyramid structure and in came a flatter team-based organization. He hated the Hudson Street building with its long corridors, closed doors, and separate reception area on each floor. The office needed a central focal point, so he smashed out a floor and built a new reception for the whole building.

Muirhead formed an executive board comprising all the top managers, showing them the most up-to-date balance sheets to try to motivate them to pull together and pull the company out of the mess. He set about resolving the rivalry still felt between the original DFS people and the Saatchi Compton people by trying to instill in them the Saatchi philosophy. In London the brothers had always acted as if their companies were bigger than they really were. Muirhead thought Saatchi's in New York needed some of the arrogance of Charlotte Street to effect real recovery. "I took to America everything I had learned from my years of working with the brothers in London," he said. "I wanted the people who worked for Saatchi to feel special in the same way that people in Charlotte Street felt special."

One afternoon not long after he arrived in New York, Muirhead decided to try an experiment. He took a colleague to stand in his newly constructed central atrium of the building and together they screamed at the tops of their voices for more than a minute. Nothing happened. Not a single door opened. "It was as if the place was dead on its feet," said Muirhead. His remedy was to take fifty of the company's most senior staff across the Hudson River to an unglamorous New Jersey conference center for three days of management soul searching, led by management consultant Bart Sale. The idea was to try to change the air of demoralization that had so permeated the building that outsiders had nicknamed it headhunters' paradise. "Things had been so bad when I arrived," said Muirhead, "that people were telling stories of Saatchi staff throwing their CVs out of windows in the hope of getting a new job." Muirhead believed the conference helped the company make a real breakthrough. "Bart specializes in helping companies that can't face up to the truth about their difficulties," he said. "It was an extremely traumatizing experience for everyone. Some people cried, some people left early, one guy even decided to leave his wife."

The process of change was slow. "Getting anything done just took forever," said Muirhead. "Even just changing the person who answered the switchboard took weeks. All I wanted was someone with a young attractive voice, but the lady who was doing it had been doing it for years and no one was used to changing things in a hurry." But presently the new approach began to reap rewards. New business was a top priority and before the end of the year Muirhead had brought in Qantas. There were still high fixed costs, as in any advertising business, but the atmosphere at Hudson Street was beginning to change. Even David Herro seemed optimistic about the future, and was quoted in an August issue of *Barron's* as believing "a year ago in the all-critical U.S. markets, two of Saatchi's three agencies were broken. Now two of the three are OK and the third is on the way back. The company has started a comeback." Muirhead was equally bullish. In an interview with London's *Evening Standard* he said, "The process is just beginning. The company, I hope, will give me a couple of years, but in my head I've given myself a year — six months to change the product and six months to get people to eat it."

When David Kershaw, Muirhead's replacement as chairman of Charlotte Street, heard about the trouble upstairs he was horrified. Kershaw looked up to Maurice Saatchi as one of the greatest admen in the world. Nineteen ninety-four had been a very successful year for the Charlotte Street agency, which had won several large accounts including all the advertising for the National Lottery. It had attracted media attention with its controversial work for the Commission for Racial Equality and a new campaign for the Army. Kershaw was looking forward to receiving his £175,000 bonus at the end of the year, and was appalled at the prospect of all his hard work being undermined by a maverick American shareholder. He might not have been present at any of Maurice's discussions with shareholders that year, he might never have spoken to David Herro before, he might be only the chairman of one small company in the group, but he wanted to have his say. He was an adman after all, he thought; he knew advertising was a people business and he thought some of these shareholders could benefit from some of his experience.

David Herro was rather taken aback by the letter that arrived from Charlotte Street on December 5. Kershaw assured him that everyone in the company had supported Maurice's share-option scheme and he argued against changing the name of the holding company. His support for the chairman was unambiguous; he claimed that Maurice's contribution alone had been a major factor in the office's profits that year. "I hope you receive these comments in the constructive spirit in which they are made," he concluded, "and my motivation in making them is only to deliver more to our clients, our employees and thereby to our shareholders." Herro immediately assumed Maurice Saatchi was behind the letter and he was furious.

As the situation continued to deteriorate, a board meeting was arranged for December 8 in New York. The day before, Bill Muirhead, from his offices at Saatchi's American headquarters, wrote to Charles Scott expressing his loyalty to Maurice: "He is cofounder of this company, and both our clients and our staff love to meet the name on the door. He is also close to many senior people in the agency, including myself. Perhaps more importantly, though, he is the human face of what is now a large multinational advertising group, without whom we would lack an obvious figurehead."

The evening before the meeting, board members and senior managers gathered for dinner in a private room at Mortimer's, one of New York's top restaurants. Maurice stood up to make a speech. He talked about the company's improved performance and his own renewed efforts to bring in new clients. The message was clear. Maurice Saatchi was working hard and shareholders would be crazy to undermine his position.

At the end of the meal Maurice left promptly, but a group of nonexecutive directors stayed on for a longer chat with some of the senior managers of Saatchi's different divisions, asking how damaging it would really be to the company if Maurice had to go. Michael Bungey, the head of Bates, had never been very close to Maurice Saatchi, who he knew was far more interested in Saatchi & Saatchi Advertising than the Bates network. He told the nonexecutives what they wanted to hear: that Maurice was probably not that crucial to the success of the business. Bill Muirhead soon excused himself from the table, uneasy at the tone of the conversation. One of the directors, Clive Gibson, took him aside and reassured him that nothing would happen to Maurice until they had spoken on the subject a second time. "I never heard from him again," says Muirhead.

The next day Saatchi & Saatchi board members met with Herro and other representatives of major shareholders, including the State of Wisconsin Investment Board, the General Electric Investment Corporation, Tiger Asset Management, and M&G Investment Management — a group whose holdings amounted to 35 percent of Saatchi stock. The board members found the shareholders adamant, demanding the removal of Maurice Saatchi and threatening to call an extraordinary general meeting and sack him themselves if the dirctors failed to act. A new meeting was arranged for December 16 in London to give everyone time to think.

On December 12 David Herro wrote to the board yet again, this time to confirm that shareholders intended to request an EGM the next week to get Maurice Saatchi removed. Jeremy Sinclair consulted Maurice and together they drew up a letter to the nonexecutives. Charles Scott, afraid of the damage that sacking the chairman might inflict on the company, also agreed to sign it. If Maurice was forced out Scott at least could tell clients he had done everything in his power to save him, he thought. The letter listed all the company's successes since the upheavals in May: the share price was up 17 percent; 1994 results were in line with market expectations; the 1995 budget showed a significant increase in revenue for the first time in four years. It even quoted David Herro in the press that summer saying Saatchi & Saatchi had "started a comeback." The letter concluded, "In our view, going back on this agreement [in May] arrived at unanimously by the Board would be to jeopardize unnecessarily these hopeful signs of progress. Therefore if a resolution is put to the Board demanding the Chairman's dismissal we could not, in the best interests of the shareholders, support it."

Wendy Smyth, the number-crunching Irish finance director of the company, refused to sign, and her name was notable by its absence. Smyth dismissed Maurice as one of the worst financial managers she had ever come across and was convinced he should resign his position as chairman of the board to concentrate on running the Saatchi & Saatchi network of advertising agencies around the world instead. As far as she could see, he was only really interested in Saatchi & Saatchi anyway. But Smyth did not know Maurice Saatchi very well. A man so accustomed to all the trappings of the chairman's position, a man who mixed with senior industrialists and politicians one day and celebrities the next, was unlikely to accept such a demotion.

Maurice suddenly realized there was real danger ahead. He had pushed hard for his share options and now he was forced to accept that they would never be granted. A new document was drawn up with superoptions based on his new salary of £200,000. He even proposed to commission a study on the advantages and disadvantages of changing the name of the holding company, conveniently ignoring the arguments put forward by Suzanna Taverne in her report. He was confident that the shareholders would have to back off again. But this time he had made a costly miscalculation. "Both brothers were opportunistic negotiators," says a former colleague. "They always wanted to see what would emerge from discussions, they instinctively knew when they had got a good deal and they always tried to push it an extra yard." Only

Maurice realized too late that he had pushed a yard too far. On December 13 the story appeared for the first time in the press. Until then, the outside world had had no idea that Maurice Saatchi was under such pressure. The shareholders were livid. Although the story could have been leaked by a number of others, they suspected Maurice, and the publicity was clearly damaging to the company. The *Financial Times*, in particular, seemed remarkably well informed of the details of Maurice's share-option scheme and the position of the protesting shareholders. The next day the other papers also carried the story: "U.S. pressure on Maurice Saatchi" ran the headline in the *Daily Telegraph*; "Saatchi faces storm over £5m options," said the *Evening Standard*.

The board started receiving messages of support for Maurice. A former nonexecutive director, Stuart Cameron, who had gone to Chicago with Sinclair and Scott the previous May to see David Herro, wrote, "Jeremy performed brilliantly at that Chicago meeting and in particular emphasized the importance of Maurice's continued contribution as Group Chairman. I wholeheartedly endorse that view." Clients were also galvanized into action. David Montgomery, chief executive of Mirror Group Newspapers, told the board, "The continuing public attacks on Maurice Saatchi, apparently by militant shareholders and some board members, are undermining the authority and standing of Saatchi's as the Mirror Group's advertising agency." Sir Colin Marshall, chairman of British Airways, wrote directly to David Herro to express his support for Maurice. But the messages served only to exacerbate the situation. David Herro and the other shareholders thought Maurice was using his relationship with the company's clients to push them into submission and it made them even more determined to get rid of him. Most of them, including Herro, ran large investment portfolios and had relatively little to lose by sacking Maurice Saatchi, even if it did result in some short-term problems for the company. The group was very high-profile, and to make an example of Maurice Saatchi would serve as an effective warning to difficult directors in other companies.

Several other problems had come to the attention of David Herro and his supporters in the weeks leading up to December 16. One was the $50,000 bill for the services of David Burnside, authorized by Bill Muirhead after senior executives in London were said to have refused to pay it. Herro was also annoyed about the lavish new offices Maurice had ordered at Charlotte Street, after he had finally vacated Berkeley Square. There were rumors that a whole corridor had been blocked off to accommodate the brothers' elaborate plans.

There was also the outstanding issue of a deal the brothers had entered into with Robert Louis-Dreyfus for shares in Adidas.

In an attempt to recruit Louis-Dreyfus to save the ailing sportswear company in 1993, he and his business partners had been offered 15 percent of Adidas's shares. The partners included Saatchi & Saatchi nonexecutive director Tom Russell, French businessman Christian Tourres, and a small U.K. investment company owned by Charles and Maurice Saatchi. Each partner put up $10,000 and the group borrowed the rest of the money to buy the shares. Before the deal was finally completed, the partners were offered the option to buy other shares in the company at a fixed price on or before January 1995. Dreyfus had been keen to bring in Charles and Maurice because of their marketing skills. Adidas might have been in difficulties, but it was still one of the most famous brand names in the business. Saatchi & Saatchi subsequently presented their advertising ideas to the company, but when they failed to win the contract, relations between the brothers and Louis-Dreyfus soured. When Louis-Dreyfus prepared to buy out the other investors, and to exclude the brothers from the deal, they took him to court and in July obtained an order to stop him. Louis-Dreyfus was trapped, as his option was due to expire at the end of the year. So in November he settled with the brothers, for $38 million. In a statement announcing the agreement, Louis-Dreyfus wrote, "I very strongly feel that, having been offered a free lunch, the Saatchis demanded the restaurant."

Shareholders, who had watched the brothers make a personal fortune from the deal, felt the money belonged to the company, arguing that they had been given such favorable terms only in return for the marketing advice they could offer Adidas in their capacity as senior directors of Saatchi & Saatchi. Tom Russell was particularly annoyed that they had made so much money from the deal. The brothers insisted that the arrangement had been a purely personal one and had nothing to do with the company. "I believe that Adidas changed everything," Bates chief executive officer Michael Bungey said in early 1995. "For the first time, Maurice had a lot of cash." Another observer said: "The Adidas payment was fuck-you money. Maurice could not have afforded to leave without it." The feeling that the brothers had got rich at the company's expense was aggravated by the article on Maurice's mansion in Sussex, featured in that month's edition of *Architectural Digest*, still making the rounds at the company.

When the meeting got under way, each of the objections to Maurice was raised in turn. As time ground on, it was becoming increasingly clear that he had only two allies left on the board, the loyal Jeremy Sinclair and a new nonexecutive director, Sir Paul Girolami, who was taking part by speaker-phone from Italy. Maurice Saatchi was waiting in a nearby office, pacing about and anxious to hear the results. Meanwhile David Herro was on holiday in the Cayman Islands. Later, much would be made in the newspapers about the American whiz kid who was sitting on the beach when Maurice Saatchi got the sack. Scott, who had signed the letter earlier in the week supporting Maurice, had changed sides, concerned, he claimed, that the threatened EGM would simply be too damaging for the company. Finally it was Jeremy Sinclair's turn to speak. "I said, 'This is a bit inconsistent,' " Sinclair recalls. " 'This spring we unanimously agreed that firing Maurice was not a good thing. All of us. Well, if it's not a good thing, you shouldn't do it.' And they said, 'Ah, but now the consequences of us not doing this bad thing will be six weeks of battle in the press prior to Herro's extraordinary general meeting, and there will be too much nasty noise. And at the EGM Maurice will be ousted anyway.' And I said, 'That may well be so, but you are not responsible for other people's actions. You will be held accountable for what you have done.' " After more debate they moved to a vote. Girolami asked how many other nonexecutives were prepared to support Maurice. When none of them came forward, he too decided to switch allegiance and Sinclair was left as the only Maurice supporter in the room. It had been decided at last; after twenty-five years, Maurice Saatchi was out.

Then came the tricky question of what the company could offer Maurice now. Since he had always loved Saatchi & Saatchi Advertising so much, it was decided that he should be offered a post as its chairman. The board said it might even agree to let him share the honorary title of life president along with his brother Charles. They could afford to be generous in victory.

Sinclair, who against his will had been voted acting

chairman, left the meeting to speak to Maurice. There was an uncomfortable silence around the table once he had closed the door behind him. When he returned, he brought the former chairman with him. Maurice was remarkably calm, telling them he would agree to accept the new position on three conditions. The first was that Sinclair should give up the role of acting chairman, which he was more than willing to do. The second was that his new contract should allow him to resign at any time without restrictions about setting up a competing agency. The board agreed. And the third was that he should receive the going rate for the job, the same as Michael Bungey, who ran Bates, and Ed Wax, the current chairman of Saatchi & Saatchi Worldwide, both of whom earned considerably more than Maurice's basic salary of £200,000 a year. The board could not agree on the final condition. Maurice returned to his office, but after another half an hour he went back into the room to tell them he had changed his mind, he couldn't agree to take the new job immediately after all, he needed time to think about it. The board gave him until January 3 to make up his mind. "Every now and then in life you get a narrow window of chance and that is what the board had then," says Sinclair. "Maurice didn't really want to leave, he loved the company, but they spent so long haggling over his salary that they blew the deal."

Meanwhile, most people at Charlotte Street had become so fed up with waiting around to hear the outcome of the board meeting that they had already gone home. David Kershaw, who still could not believe that Maurice would really be pushed out of the company, was on the way to his car when he bumped into one of the Saatchi drivers. "He told me, 'Have you heard, they've finally done it, they've shot the chairman,'" he recalls. Bill Muirhead had been to the Royal Opera House that evening. He also learned the

148

news from one of the company drivers, who had been sent to pick him up afterwards. He immediately spoke to Maurice by phone and remembers him sounding very quiet, as if he were calling long-distance. They talked about the other job he had been offered and Muirhead told Maurice he should take it.

Two days later David Kershaw, Bill Muirhead, and Jeremy Sinclair — the three amigos, as they were eventually dubbed by the press — held a crisis meeting in Sinclair's office at Charlotte Street. Together they drafted a note for the staff. "As you probably know," it read, "Maurice Saatchi ceased to be chairman of Saatchi & Saatchi PLC on Friday. He is currently considering an offer to be the chairman of Saatchi & Saatchi Advertising Worldwide. We all hope he will accept this offer and we urge anyone who agrees to encourage him to stay. In the meantime, it is important to stress that it is business as usual. It is absolutely critical that our clients do not feel that we are distracted from producing great advertising for them. Now more than ever the Saatchi agencies need to over-service and over-deliver."

Sinclair was very depressed. He had fought so hard for Maurice, and now the company would be faced, he was sure, with big problems from angry clients. "Advertising is the kind of business where you need to be on the attack, the winning side; it's extremely difficult when the management's on the back foot," he says. "I despaired of spending a year sorting out all the problems. Who needs it? I thought." Sinclair was convinced he was surrounded by people on the board who had no integrity, who promised one thing one minute and changed their minds the next. He is a man who prides himself on his principles; if Maurice decided not to stay, he would leave too. He told the other two of his decision. They also said they did not want to continue working for

Saatchi & Saatchi without Maurice. The three discussed setting up their own agency together. They called Maurice at home to see if he had decided what to do. He told them he had thought about the offer, but he knew he would probably have to leave. "My thinking was, it was a great job," he says. "I've heard people say it was a demeaning job. I didn't think it was demeaning at all. What could be better than being chairman of Saatchi & Saatchi? But if Saatchi & Saatchi was to be owned by David Herro, I decided in the end, I couldn't do it."

Over the next few days Maurice was inundated with requests from people at Saatchi & Saatchi, pleading with him to stay. Most of them knew nothing of the shareholders' complex web of objections, many had never even met Maurice themselves. But Maurice Saatchi represented something about the agency at its world-conquering best that commanded their loyalty. "Please join us as our chairman and leader," came the emotional appeal.

Christmas was fast approaching and the three amigos decided to consult their lawyers, seeking advice on their contracts to find out how difficult it would be to free themselves if they decided to resign. For now there was nothing else to do but to take their Christmas holidays, each heading off in a different direction with the same plan of action: first, they would continue to try and persuade Maurice to stay; second, if that proved impossible, they would resign from the company themselves; and third, they would go into partnership together.

The three were still on holiday on the third of January, when Maurice Saatchi finally told the company he was leaving, expressing his feelings in a terse little memo to the board: "Please inform Mr. Herro that I do not accept his offer. It was kind of him to consider me for the position."

To the staff at the company there was a rather longer explanation. He told them that the "enforced parting grieves me deeply" and went on, "Saatchi & Saatchi has been taken over. No premium has been paid. No shareholder vote has been taken, but, make no mistake, Saatchi & Saatchi is under new control. The new 'owners' — a group of shareholders owning around 30 percent of the shares — have found a simple if crude method of controlling the company. By threatening the directors with an extraordinary general meeting — at which they could outvote the others — they have given the directors their orders: 'Take the chairman into a corner and shoot him quietly — we don't want the fuss of a public trial.' "

In fact, there were no new owners of the company; Charles and Maurice had long since sold their controlling shares. There was no new bid for the company; this was simply the shareholders exercising their rights. But Maurice Saatchi was not the man to take his shooting quietly. He wanted revenge. "The level of rage," said Tim Bell at the time, "is extraordinary." Maurice ended his letter on an ominous note: "Yet I look forward to 1995 with great anticipation. Because, as we have always believed at Saatchi & Saatchi . . . Nothing is Impossible."

As soon as the letter was made public, newspapers around the world went into a fury of speculation. Was Maurice planning to set up a rival agency? Did he really have the energy and drive needed to start again from scratch? How would Saatchi's clients react to his departure? What would happen to the old company? Only *Private Eye* greeted Maurice Saatchi's exit with equanimity: "Man with Glasses Leaves Job" screamed a mock tabloid headline in the magazine's January 13 issue. There had already been reports that Mars had begun talking to some of Saatchi's rivals. Now it was announced that the Conservative Party was also reviewing its relationship with the company. Even Maurice himself was taken aback by the level of media interest in his story. He phoned the amigos at their respective holiday hotels. He was considering the possibility of working in politics, or setting up a consultancy. He might even think of establishing a new advertising agency. The three told him of their plans to go it alone; Maurice could join them as an equal partner. They all arranged to meet at Maurice's London house in Bruton Place the following Sunday evening.

On the way back to London Muirhead flew to New York to collect his personal belongings and take one last look at the building; it would be the last time he ever went inside. He had been the head of the troubled New York office for less than a year. The next day he met the other two at David Kershaw's flat in Kensington and they took a cab together to Maurice's house. Negotiations went on for some time, but until a provisional agreement had been hammered out everyone was determined not to accept a drink. Charles was also present, though he would still be an employee of Saatchi & Saatchi for some time yet, so his intended involvement in the future agency was to be kept top secret.

At last they were agreed. Maurice, Charles, Sinclair, Kershaw, and Muirhead would each own a fifth of the company around the world. In every country where they had an office, local managers would also be able to hold a small stake. Josephine Hart opened a bottle of wine to drink a toast to their new partnership. "Maurice likes his wine very cold indeed," says Sinclair, "and that evening it was almost icy. Apparently, if the temperature is low enough, the water in the wine freezes and makes it much more alcoholic, which perhaps explains why we all seemed to be drunk after just half a glass that night."

*C*RANKS, AN UNEXCEPTIONAL HEALTH-FOOD CAFÉ on Tottenham Street just around the corner from Saatchi & Saatchi's offices in Fitzrovia, is an unlikely place to spot three of the country's most senior admen huddled together over morning coffee and toast. But on January 9, 1995, the three amigos — David Kershaw, Jeremy Sinclair, and Bill Muirhead — were nervously watching the world go by from their table at the window and reading one another's resignation letters. Each had spent hours carefully choosing his words to Charles Scott. Sinclair spoke for them all when he wrote, "The Company is in the grip of people who do not understand the business and seem prepared to ignore the advice of those who do." He had added, "I never intended to leave the Company, but it seems the Company has left me."

That morning, Jeremy Sinclair was unsettled by the prospect of the enormous step he was about to take. The adman who had worked for Charles Saatchi ever since leaving Watford Art College in 1968 had always told his friends that he would never leave Saatchi & Saatchi. ("He used to say he only wanted one job and one wife," a former colleague recalls.) The other two amigos had thirty-five years' experience at Saatchi & Saatchi between them, and so the prospect of resigning was difficult for Muirhead and Kershaw too. "It was a bit like an out-of-body experience. We couldn't really believe we were there," remembers Muirhead. Sinclair had one last coffee before the three walked the couple of hundred yards down the street to the agency's offices. Hardly noticing the visitors sitting in the reception, they took the elevator to Charles Scott's office. It was twelve noon precisely.

Scott was expecting to see Sinclair at midday. Sinclair had requested the appointment the previous week and Scott had assumed they were going to discuss the best way to limit the damage of Maurice's abrupt and very public departure. There was a knock on the door. He put aside the papers he had been working on and looked up from his desk, surprised to see that Kershaw and Muirhead also seemed to have invited themselves to the meeting. Scott was taken aback by their resignation letters. The amigos had never given him any indication that they would leave if Maurice were removed from the company, and he was angry that they had never warned him.

"It was as if he was in shock, finding himself at the center of such a drama," says Sinclair. "He asked us if there was anything he could say that would make us stay." The three told him they had made up their minds, that they could not continue to work for a company that no longer seemed to care about its clients' opinions or its staff morale, even if Scott himself offered to resign — which he did.

"We couldn't have told him we would resign if Maurice was sacked," insists Muirhead. "It would have been like blackmail, and if I had been in Scott's shoes I would have immediately moved the people threatening me to a position where they couldn't do any damage in the future. It could have marked the end of our careers at Saatchi & Saatchi if we had decided to stay."

Scott told them their decision would do yet more damage to the very company they professed to love so much, leading to lay-offs among its staff. Sinclair was angry. He told Scott he was still disgusted at the way Maurice had been treated. The shareholders had acted dishonorably and could never be trusted again, he said. Scott recognized that he would not be able to persuade them to change their minds. After asking them to recommend their replacements, he slumped back wearily in his chair as the three left his office and walked back through reception and out of Charlotte Street for the last time. They hailed a cab around the corner on Tottenham Court Road and directed it to the Langham Hilton Hotel for a meeting they had arranged with their own newly appointed publicity men.

David Kershaw had left the day-to-day running of Charlotte Street in the hands of his two deputies, Moray McLennan and Nick Hurrell, while he had been on holiday over Christmas. Both were in their early thirties and had been promoted to the post of joint managing directors less than a year before. They had arrived for work as normal on the morning of Monday, January 9. At nine-thirty the phone rang; it was Maurice Saatchi. He told them he would like to talk to them and asked them to visit him at Bruton Place around midday. They agreed and at the appointed time they took a cab to Mayfair, where they were shown immediately into Maurice's study. The offer of jobs in a new Saatchi agency came as a surprise. "My mind just raced off into millions of questions about all the pros and cons," recalls McLennan. "We said we would consider it, that it could be very exciting and so forth, but that it would be a very big decision and we needed time to think."

Maurice asked them to let him know as soon as possible the next day and they hurried back to the agency. McLennan had a lunch appointment with a client from Schweppes and he was already half an hour late.

Hurrell and McLennan were not the only visitors that morning at Bruton Place. The agency's two creative directors, James Lowther and Simon Dicketts, had also had a call from Maurice Saatchi that morning, and when they arrived at his house he made them the same offer of attractive jobs with the new company. Equally surprised and very flattered, they walked around the corner to Mortons, a private club on Berkeley Square. "We sat there and just said 'Blimey' a lot and agreed at least as far as it was possible to stick together," recalled Dicketts afterwards. The offer was especially difficult for Simon Dicketts to absorb. He had been away at his mother's funeral during the boardroom row in December and had returned to work the previous week with other things on his mind. As the afternoon wore on, they started to draw up a list of advantages and disadvantages. Later they went on to Lowther's house in Chelsea to continue to talk, without returning to the agency at all that day.

Back in Charlotte Street, Charles Scott was conducting a crisis meeting of all the senior managers left in the building, including Wendy Smyth, Saatchi's financial director, Michael Bungey, head of Bates, Derek Bowden, head of Saatchi's in Europe, and (still unaware of their conversation with Maurice Saatchi at lunchtime) McLennan and Hurrell. On the phone from New York were Ed Wax, the head of the Saatchi & Saatchi Advertising network, and other senior managers at Saatchi's American subsidiaries. Scott told them all about the amigos' resignations that morning and then, turning to McLennan and Hurrell, said it was impossible for him to make any decisions about the future of the company until he could be sure of their loyalty. "We need time to take all this in," McLennan remembers telling him. "Even if you offered me the most tremendous deal possible to stay at this company for the next two years, I'm not sure I could sign it at the moment. The fact is I'm just not sure I want to work for a company which has done either stupid or devious things."

Scott, the usually placid chief executive, was on the edge of losing his temper for the second time that day. As somebody else who was at the meeting recalls, "He told them it was obvious that there were a few things they didn't understand. He started to talk about Maurice, about his financial mismanagement of the company, which had brought it to the brink of bankruptcy. He told them how much company money Maurice had wasted on gardeners and butlers, how he had insisted on staying in offices in Berkeley Square despite the cost. He went on and on."

Then Scott went around the room asking for everyone's ideas on the company's best next move. Hurrell and McLennan were in a very difficult position. They told him what they knew he was expecting to hear, that they must think of the clients first, which meant, they said, refusing to accept the resignations of their former colleagues Sinclair, Kershaw, and Muirhead and seeing how long they could hold them to their contracts. There was general agreement around the table. Charles Scott knew it was his duty to inform the City of the news before it leaked out elsewhere, but he was also aware that it would rock the company's share price yet again, and he wanted to leave the statement until the last possible minute. "He seemed to have so much on his mind, he could barely decide what to do first," says an insider. Finally, just before four-thirty, Scott left the room to make the stock-market announcement before the markets closed, just minutes before the news would appear on the front page of the *Evening Standard*.

McLennan and Hurrell returned to their offices, each sitting behind his desk in despair. They made a few calls to clients, most of whom wanted to know if they were going to leave the company too. They tried to reassure everyone, including members of the staff who came to see them at the end of the afternoon. After an hour, the strain was beginning to show. In McLennan's office the phone rang. It was Simon Dicketts. "I asked him if he had spoken to Maurice and he told me he had," says Dicketts. "We both felt we had a lot of unanswered questions. We both felt we were faced with a really big decision. We decided all four of us should meet up at James Lowther's house in Chelsea that evening. At one in the morning we were still talking.' "

"It was an incredibly difficult decision," recalled McLennan afterwards. "On the one hand, you just felt so responsible for all the people at the agency you would leave behind if you decided to go, but, on the other, it was clear that joining Maurice was probably the best thing we could do for ourselves. The problem, if we stayed, was we would have to tell people, 'Work hard, keep your head down, we'll be fine. We'll even be rich and famous and the world will be wonderful,' but I knew I'd feel such a hypocrite saying such things. Realistically, we had seen Charles Scott and the other managers behave irresponsibly, in our opinion, and who could tell what else they might do in the future. It seemed likely then that clients would leave as a result of Maurice's sacking and there was nothing we could have done to prevent it. In fact, we could have encouraged the whole agency to work really hard, just to find Charles Scott and his cronies cutting our legs off through some action or other I couldn't foresee.

"It just seemed easier to go, but, on the other hand, the agency was in chaos and what I was leaving behind frightened me. It gave me no pleasure at all to think about people running around and panicking if we left them to it. But then again, did this mean I could never leave the company? It was a terrible dilemma, the decision was so hard, but by the early hours of the morning all four of us had agreed we would probably leave. We were tired and overwrought and so Simon, Nick, and I went home to sleep on it."

The decision could have gone either way that night, according to Simon Dicketts. "We were optimistic that if we all stayed we could probably hold the agency together and that gave us a tremendous sense of power," he says, "but the more we talked about it, the more inevitable it seemed that we were going to leave."

The next morning McLennan and Hurrell, then Dicketts and Lowther, went to see Maurice to finalize details of their new contracts. All four, in common with most senior advertising people in the same position, wanted to make sure they would have some equity in the company. Maurice reassured them that they would have a stake in the London operation. By lunchtime they had agreed to join him, although nothing was formally signed.

Hurrell and McLennan went back to the office. By early afternoon their situation was becoming intolerable. People were saying that they should be talking to the press and calling a staff meeting, trying to answer all the difficult questions. McLennan called Maurice and told him it was too difficult to stay there a minute longer. "I told him, 'In another hour I will have committed myself to helping sort out the mess and I won't be able to break my word,'" he says. "I told my secretary I was going out, but she knew what was really happening. It was a very odd feeling, just walking out without being able to say good-bye, knowing I was never going to work in that building again."

McLennan and Hurrell met late that afternoon at their lawyer's offices with the papers from Maurice and signed on the dotted line. Dicketts and Lowther, meanwhile, had still not been back to the office. They too met their lawyers and signed up with the new Saatchi agency.

It had been a day of speculation for the press, most of which had reported Monday's three resignations at length. *The Evening Standard,* which had printed the amigos' resignation letters in full, reported that Maurice Saatchi was behind a plot to devastate Saatchi & Saatchi so that its share price would sink low enough for the brothers to buy it back privately. It was true that the share price was sinking: £33 million had been wiped off as a result of the resignations of Kershaw, Sinclair, and Muirhead. It also emerged that Maurice and Charles Saatchi had sold their remaining shares in the company a few days before Monday's defections. A friend of Maurice defended him by saying that he had decided to sell his shares as soon as he was ousted, well before he knew that his three colleagues would also be leaving the agency. At Charlotte Street, Charles Scott, now acting chairman as well as chief executive of the holding company, moved quickly to appoint Ed Wax and Michael Bungey to the board. As expected, Alan Bishop, Muirhead's deputy in New York, was named as the man to take over from him. In an official statement Scott said he was very disappointed that the three defectors had decided to leave the company. "Individually, they have contributed greatly to the Saatchi & Saatchi Advertising network," he said. As the day progressed the share price fell from 124 pence at the end of trading on Monday to 109 pence.

Lord King, president of British Airways and one of Maurice's most loyal contacts, had written to the *Daily Telegraph* that morning. In December he had privately warned the board of Saatchi & Saatchi that he was very unhappy about threats to remove Maurice Saatchi from the agency. Now he chose to make his views public.

"The recent events at Saatchi & Saatchi, an agency with which British Airways has enjoyed an excellent relationship since 1982, raise important issues of corporate governance. Are we to believe that a Chicago-based institution, owning less than 10 per cent of the company's stock, is able to dominate board policy in the United Kingdom? It has never been made clear how much of Saatchi & Saatchi's stock Mr. David Herro, of Harris Associates, actually spoke for. Was it 30 per cent, 40 per cent or 49.9 per cent? Any such figure would still represent a minority. Mr. Herro originally challenged Maurice Saatchi's proposed share-option agreement, which was not put to all the shareholders, but latterly he called for Mr. Saatchi's removal from the chair. How many of the vocal minority were in agreement with this change of emphasis, which carried far more damaging implications? Were all the minority in favor of all the proposals, including the change of the company's name, which, after all, has proved good enough to attract the Government?"

The next day Lowther and Dicketts decided they wanted to get their resignations over as quickly as possible. Early in the morning they went into Charlotte Street the back way, through the official holding-company entrance, and took the elevator up to Charles Scott's office. This time Scott was better prepared for the bad news. The meeting lasted an hour. He did not try to talk them out of leaving or ask them about their future plans. All he wanted to know was why they were going. "I told him I really admired

Jeremy and just couldn't imagine working there without him," says Dicketts. "I said I thought the agency was now being run by people who knew nothing about advertising." Scott knew there was nothing he could say to persuade them to stay, and Dicketts and Lowther left his office together. But when they returned to their car, parked outside the agency, they found it had been clamped. "It was a nightmare," says Dicketts. "All we wanted to do was drive away as quickly as possible, but instead both James and I were sitting inside, on our mobile phones, trying to get someone to unclamp us." Saatchi employees still arriving for work found the spectacle highly amusing.

An hour later, Hurrell and McLennan arrived at Charles Scott's door to hand in their resignations. Scott was becoming accustomed to accepting resignation letters by now. He told them he was still angry about the abrupt departure of Jeremy Sinclair, Bill Muirhead, and David Kershaw. "He told us he thought they had acted very badly," remembers McLennan. "He said he understood it was their right to stop working for one company and start working for another, but he insisted they had still behaved very badly in resigning in the way they had. After that he even wished us good luck and let us walk around the agency to say a few good-byes.

"The only time I ever regretted leaving Saatchi's was during that first week," McLennan says. "One minute I'd had this big air-conditioned office, with people running around for me and enormous bonuses in the pipeline, and the next I had no routine in my life at all. We knew if we had stayed we would probably have been offered the chairman and chief executive role at Charlotte Street. Then I thought I couldn't stay there forever. I was always going to leave at some point. But it was a difficult place to leave, really difficult, because it had been like a family."

On Wednesday David Herro made a reappearance, this time in the British press. "Maurice Saatchi was today dismissed as a brilliant adman with no business sense in an astonishing attack by the man who forced him out of his agency and brought it to the brink of crisis," said a report in the *Evening Standard*. "American fund holder David Herro said Maurice was 'rolling around like a drunken sailor' buying everything in sight and had to be stopped before he bankrupted the company. And Mr. Herro claimed that 80 per cent of Saatchi shareholders agreed with him. But with Maurice out of the way Mr. Herro . . . rising star of Chicago-based Harris Associates, believes Saatchi & Saatchi will make a complete recovery."

At the same time, the company was receiving heavy blows from its clients. Both British Airways and Mirror Group Newspapers confirmed on Wednesday that they were reviewing their advertising accounts with the agency. Robert Ayling, British Airways' managing director, wrote to Charles Scott: "In view of the uncertainty arising from recent events . . . I have asked for a general review to be carried out," but he added that, in theory at least, Saatchi & Saatchi could still win back the account. Mirror Group announced that it was definitely taking its advertising account, with an estimated £10 million a year in billings, away from Saatchi & Saatchi, complaining that the company had "ignored" its concerns about Maurice Saatchi's removal. Scott could hardly claim to be surprised at these two decisions. Maurice was known to be close both to Lord King at BA and to David Montgomery, the former editor of *Today* and now the head of Mirror Group. When Montgomery had been out of a job several years before, Bill Muirhead, running Charlotte Street at the time, had offered him the free use of an office, and Montgomery did not forget such favors quickly. Stanley Kalms, chairman of the electrical retail group Dixons and another of Saatchi & Saatchi's clients, also chose Wednesday to make public his concerns about the recent events at the agency. Saying he intended to take a fresh look at his company's advertising needs, he told the *Financial Times*, "I'm most uncomfortable about the method of Maurice's enforced departure." Dixons spent an estimated £40 million a year on advertising through the agency.

Wednesday was the day Maurice decided to announce officially that he intended to set up a rival advertising agency with his three partners, Jeremy Sinclair, Bill Muirhead, and David Kershaw. "I have been called by many clients who wish to know my plans," he said. "In order to avoid any more uncertainty, I have decided to announce the foundation of a new agency." Saatchi & Saatchi attempted to reassure the world that it still had everything under control by releasing part of a statement Scott had made to investors and analysts in Europe and America. "This company is still run by people who understand advertising and the other businesses which Saatchi operates," he said.

In three days, the press coverage of Saatchi & Saatchi had reached excessive levels. As public relations supremo Tim Bell led the offensive for Maurice, every national newspaper apart from the *Daily Mail* decided that Monday's resignations of Sinclair, Muirhead, and Kershaw were more important than either political infighting in the Labour Party or the Russian bombardment of Chechnya. ITN's *News at Ten* had even sent a team to sit outside the agency on Monday night to try to interview worried employees at the agency on their way home. Notices had been posted in Saatchi & Saatchi's reception area asking staff not to speak to the press.

By then the company had started hitting back. It accused Maurice of taking filing cabinets containing confidential papers and keeping them at an address in north London. It threatened publicly to sue him for the return of the papers and to sue all former employees if they started up as rivals before their contracts had expired. Maurice returned twenty-one crates of papers after the threat, but retained those he regarded as his personal property.

There were more rumors that the Conservative Party was looking at ways to withdraw its account from the agency. It was revealed, however, that the party still had to repay a secret £600,000 loan from the agency, as part of unpaid fees run up at Saatchi & Saatchi during the 1992 election campaign. Michael Dobbs, deputy Conservative Party chairman, said, "It's a problem which is one for the agency at the moment, not the Conservative Party. We are simply sitting back and looking at what happens." Party chairman Jeremy Hanley, however, was understood to have asked for legal advice on whether the departure of key people who worked on its account at the agency, like Maurice and Jeremy Sinclair, breached the Conservatives' contract. But the issue was not a pressing one. The Tories make little use of their advertising agency outside election campaigns, apart from some occasional advice on policy presentations and the odd party political broadcast. There would be relatively little advertising work required for the local elections in May and it could probably be handled by less experienced people at the agency. From Saatchi & Saatchi's perspective, the battle for the Conservative account was more about prestige than cash, but at a time when the agency appeared to be going into meltdown, every potential account loss was making the front pages.

Scott had been quick to appoint new managers for the

Charlotte Street office. Derek Bowden, a quiet-spoken, low-profile former media man, stepped into the breach. After consulting Scott and Ed Wax, who had flown into London on Tuesday, he chose two very young and very inexperienced people to run the London office until a new chairman could be found to replace David Kershaw. Tamara Ingram had been considered for the job of managing director the year before, when Hurrell and McLennan were appointed. Thirty-four years old, she had spent virtually all her ten years at Saatchi & Saatchi working for the agency's most important but also most conventional client, Procter & Gamble. Senior managers had felt then that she needed more experience with a wider range of accounts before she could be promoted. But now it was crucial to the future of Charlotte Street that P&G be kept happy, and having their account manager in charge would certainly help. *Campaign* described her as "strong, dynamic and confident" and claimed she was "steeped in Saatchi culture." Adam Crozier, on the other hand, had for seven years been working his way up through the agency's media department, rather as Tim Bell had done but lacking Bell's charisma. He was a nondescript, steady worker who, at thirty-one, had worked on a variety of accounts from Toyota to Mirror Group. The pair's first job was to appoint replacements for Lowther and Dicketts in the creative department. Cliff Francis, aged thirty-seven, who had been at the agency for fifteen years, Richard Myers, forty-five and a Saatchi man for twenty years, and Adam Kean, thirty-three and with eight years, were all appointed joint creative directors. One former insider expressed his doubts about the new setup: "I don't know how inspirational this team is. . . . The Saatchi culture seems to be vanishing. It's in danger of becoming just another multinational agency."

On Wednesday, their first day as joint chief executives, Ingram and Crozier did little but talk to journalists. "It was absolutely shattering," said Crozier later. "I think that week I must have gone through the full range of emotions, from shock on Monday, to a feeling of unreality on Tuesday, Wednesday more shock, and by the end of the week anger with Maurice Saatchi and his announcement that he was setting up an agency."

That evening the new managers decided to hold a staff party in the company bar, the Pregnant Man. It was the first chance for the agency's five hundred or so employees to take a break from the crisis. "At the party everyone was clapping," remembered Ingram. "It felt that we were all sticking together. What people from the outside have never understood about the agency is that it really never has been about just one or two people."

Scott and Bowden were both aware that Ingram and Crozier would need the support of older, more experienced managers. They thought of Marilyn Baxter, who had originally joined Saatchi & Saatchi in 1986, then left after six years to sail around the world. A down-to-earth woman best known for publishing an analysis of sexual harassment in advertising, she had never really had much respect for Maurice Saatchi. She had been back in the country only a matter of weeks when she got a call from Derek Bowden asking her to come in and see him. By five-thirty on Wednesday afternoon she had been appointed head of client services and she started work immediately, leaving for home that night after midnight.

All the news was too much for the share price, which lurched again on Thursday, down more than 10 percent to a new record low of 96 pence. Charles Scott hit out in that week's *Campaign* at what he described as an "organized and cynical" advance publicity campaign for Maurice Saatchi's new agency. He promised to hold all the senior defectors to their contracts. For the three amigos, this meant in theory that they could be banned from working for any other agency for several years. For Hurrell, McLennan, Dicketts, and Lowther the restrictions could stretch from three to twelve months. Maurice, of course, was free to begin work immediately, since he had been effectively sacked from the agency. There were Saatchi stories all over the front page of the magazine. Characteristically, the news of Maurice's new agency took precedence over Saatchi & Saatchi's attempts to control the damage. The diary column offered readers a bottle of champagne for the best idea for a new name for Saatchi & Saatchi now one of the Saatchis had left. Suggestions included Bates and Bean-counters Worldwide, Saacked and Saackies, Herro and Good-bye, and Saatchi minus Saatchi.

While the British press was almost unanimous in its support of Maurice Saatchi, the glamorous and somewhat mysterious adman ousted in a boardroom battle with his company's so-called bean-counters, in the United States it was a different story.

Advertising Age, the industry's leading trade magazine, was unequivocal in its condemnation of Maurice. In a front page editorial it thundered: "We abhor what Maurice Saatchi has done and what he seems determined to do now by starting this new agency. We urge the current management of Saatchi & Saatchi Co. to protect its rights with every legal means at its disposal. Further, we strongly urge Saatchi clients to avoid another dangerous and bumpy ride on the wild side at the 'new' Saatchi."

At *ADWEEK,* the verdict was hardly more encouraging.

"The Saatchi brothers might be admired in the U.K., but people see things differently here," it said. "Maurice Saatchi is not as legendary as he is notorious. The aura that surrounded Saatchi's Charlotte Street offices was never exported here. Saatchi is someone who took money from money managers and bought his way to the biggest. And when he made a mess of it, continued to flaunt his image and corporate lifestyle in the board's face."

On Thursday night Maurice invited the entire thirty-strong British Airways team at Charlotte Street to his house for cocktails, confident, even then, that his new agency would win the airline's prestigious advertising account. Of course, he could not offer them jobs immediately, but when rumors of the evening leaked out the next day it was said that he had asked them all to resign en masse to join the new company. "It was nonsense," said Crozier later. "After all, he had nothing definite to offer them. All it succeeded in doing was annoying British Airways."

Scott stepped in again to try and calm the situation with a statement, this time to all City and news editors: "To date, a total of seven staff have resigned since the New Year, out of a total workforce of about 11,000 worldwide. All these worked within the Saatchi & Saatchi Advertising Worldwide network. All but one worked in the London agency office of the network. No other operating units within the group are affected. Saatchi and Saatchi Advertising Ltd. is the London agency office of the Saatchi & Saatchi Advertising Worldwide network. Its annual revenues are less than 20 per cent of the Saatchi & Saatchi Advertising Worldwide network as a whole. It employs approximately 550 people." By Friday a very angry Saatchi & Saatchi had started to take serious action against the defectors. Legal writs were issued against Sinclair, Muirhead, Kershaw, and Maurice Saatchi, accusing them of conspiring to injure the company, and against Maurice for soliciting the other three. Saatchi & Saatchi was also seeking to prevent Sinclair, Muirhead, and Kershaw from joining a rival business, or soliciting or working for Saatchi & Saatchi clients in such a business, and was looking for damages for breach of contract.

The weekend newspapers were full of Saatchi news. The *Sunday Times* carried a piece entitled "Maurice Versus the Bean-Counters." It concluded: "Maurice, at least in the early stages of the Saatchi versus Saatchi confrontation, was making all the running." The paper also claimed in its Business Section that angry U.S. investors were planning to take legal action against the directors of Saatchi & Saatchi, saying that the value of their shareholding had been damaged by the departure of Maurice Saatchi. It was true that by the end of that week £115 million had been wiped off the company's market capitalization since the board meeting on December 16. One of Saatchi & Saatchi's nonexecutive directors, Tom Russell, accused Maurice Saatchi in the *Independent on Sunday* of mismanagement on a massive scale. "Maurice was very expensive. As a member of the compensation committee, I can tell you some of his expenses were egregious," he said. And Charlotte Street hit back at Maurice in its own fashion with a full-page advertisement carried in the *Sunday Times* quoting parts of the resignation letters to staff by their former managers. It ran sentences from the memos that had praised the company, under the headline: "The first advertisement created by the people who've just left Saatchi & Saatchi."

ten NEW SAATCHI

*T*HE NEW SAATCHI AGENCY started life on the third floor of an anonymous office building behind Oxford Street. The name on the door was Dress Rehearsal, but everyone in the advertising business knew this was the new headquarters of Maurice Saatchi. With its cheap carpets, mass-produced black furniture, and plastic potted plants, Davies Street was a far cry from the luxury and seclusion of the brothers' Berkeley Square offices. A sign of the times, it was as though Maurice was taking a lead from his former protégé Martin Sorrell, now head of WPP, whose London offices were designed to look more productive than luxurious. "The world has changed," Maurice concedes. "This is the caring nineties. I walked around for years wearing two balls and a chain attached to my legs at all times. One ball had on it 'Icon of Thatcherism' and the other ball had on it 'Eighties Excess.' I've grown quite attached to them."

In the offices of New Saatchi, the sort of efficient modern workspace that instantly makes you feel that you have no right to be among its purposeful occupants with their clipboards and their deadlines, Maurice Saatchi himself could be seen mingling with the rest of the small staff of loyal employees as he stepped between his cramped office, the makeshift boardroom, and the coffee machine, his Savile Row–tailored personal assistant, James Stuart, in constant attendance. He showed no sign of being engaged in the struggle of his career. Perhaps it was because Davies Street had a few saving graces. Situated almost next door to Claridge's, it was just five minutes away from Berkeley Square itself. Maurice Saatchi thought that the management of the old company would probably have liked the unflamboyant atmosphere of Davies Street. "Their view was that it was important to look shabby to please the shareholders," he says. "Well, you can have some very happy shareholders, but if you don't have any clients you will be living in shabby circumstances, because you're not going to have any income."

From behind his new desk, Maurice Saatchi was still throwing himself into the role of the tragic hero undone by the machinations of a ruthless American fiend. Predictably, the question of his notorious expenses operated as a leitmotif in the Saatchi monologues. "Chairmen of public companies do business entertaining," he intoned. "They take people out. They organize events. They take groups of people to the opera or the theater, or have cocktail parties. That's what chairmen do with their customers. That's what I do. That was part of my job. So, yes, if a company like this one — which is in the hands of people who have somehow to rationalize that they've halved the share price and lost half a billion dollars of business, and the best they can muster is, 'What an expensive fellow. Dear, oh dear.' To me, that is the absolute last refuge. It's pathetic."

In fact, Maurice Saatchi discovered that he was more in demand as a result of his ousting than he had been for years. He could spend hours chatting with potential new clients, or fielding reporters' questions, while trying to charm the best people from "Oldco," his new name for his former company, into joining him. Every now and then Tim Bell would phone, updating Maurice on the latest barrage of calls from the press. The former Saatchi "third brother" estimated that, at the height of the media's interest, he was fielding between 100 and 120 calls a day from journalists around the world.

The fact that Bell was helping to coordinate Maurice and Charles's public relations effort was remarkable in itself, according to Paul Bainsfair. "Deep down perhaps Tim loved to have the brothers needing him and wanting him," he says. "Perhaps coming to the rescue like that met some unfulfilled need he had." In any case, Charles concedes that he and Maurice would have struggled to get their message across without the help of their old friend. "Tim was phenomenal," he adds. "He's got very good judgment about what is tasteless and what is OK. When you're being shat on and lots of horrible things are being said about you, it's easy to crack. Without Tim around, we would have fucked it up."

Maurice's enemies claimed that the brothers were using the £38 million they had won from Louis-Dreyfus in the Adidas settlement to fund the New Saatchi, and so, inevitably, the old Saatchi put in motion a suit to get the money back. Across town there was rather less activity at the makeshift offices of the three amigos — or the three egos, as some people in the advertising business were now calling them. Sinclair, Kershaw, and Muirhead were on "gardening leave," still paid by the old company though not working there, and unable to work for the new agency until they had freed themselves from their contracts. Together they rented themselves a base in the West End where they could meet during the coming months of involuntary idleness. The potting shed, as they called it, was in actuality a small flat complete with kitchen and bathroom on the top floor of an apartment building on Sackville Street, just off Piccadilly. A plain black boardroom table was installed in what should have been the bedroom. Around it the three full-time gardeners complete with designer suits and mobile phones gathered each day to talk about what they described as the apocalyptic events of the past few weeks.

The three amigos were enjoying themselves. Sitting around the office on Sackville Street for days on end, they felt like upright men of integrity who had taken the brave, some would say even heroic, step of leaving Saatchi & Saatchi in the interests of truth, justice, and loyalty. They held the management of Oldco in contempt. Charles Scott was regarded by them as a turncoat who had changed sides at the crucial moment. David Herro was the megalomaniac shareholder who had led the Furies against Maurice. Oldco was doomed; it was just a matter of time until all its biggest clients abandoned it. Maurice had been right in his resignation letter to condemn the so-called financial experts. What did they know? You had only to look at what had happened to the share price since he had been ousted from the chairmanship to see the damage that had been done to the company, they told each other.

These meditations were interrupted from time to time by teams of lawyers who were working overtime to put together statements from the amigos that would form part of their defense against Saatchi & Saatchi in court. Important documents were stashed away in the closet in what should have been the bedroom of the flat. "We suddenly had to get interested in things we knew nothing about, like swearing affidavits and discussing interlocutory hearings," says Sinclair. "It was like learning to play Scrabble for the first time. In a way it did have its own fascination."

After a couple of weeks the Sackville Three began to tire of the legal formalities. They were admen, after all, and they were proud of it. They wanted to get on and start working at the new company, but their hands were tied. All they could do was talk to media-buying companies about possible linkups with the new agency, investigate international advertising networks that might be interested in working with them later in the year, and start the search for proper offices for New Saatchi. But most of the time they just sat around on Sackville Street, dressed up in their best suits, making one another cups of coffee, talking to the press, and calling their friends.

Outside their secluded little gardening shed, the advertising industry was horrified by the unfolding drama. After years of struggle to shake off the industry's reputation for ego, flashiness, showbiz, and hubris, the high-profile posturings of Maurice Saatchi and companions were considered disastrous. Adland, still desperate for the professional status sought thirty years before by men like David Ogilvy, craved respectability. This was a business still crawling out of a deep recession, and many echoed the views of Chris Powell, one of the elder statesman of the industry and chairman of rival agency BMP DDB Needham, when he said, "The bust-up has done the industry's standing no good to the outside world. It's a distraction." John Tylee, a journalist on *Campaign,* wrote, "The only certainty is that the struggle to win the PR battle has served only to reinforce media and public prejudice against people seen as 'all style and no substance,'" adding, "This tacky affair does no favors to an industry trying to present itself as the economy's lubricating oil, helping to sustain company profits and jobs."

Charles Saatchi decided to take matters into his own hands, as the only Saatchi brother still on the payroll at Saatchi & Saatchi. He approached the management of the company with an offer he hoped would bring peace to the warring factions. Using an intermediary at the company's merchant bankers, Charles suggested that the group agree to offer his brother a place on the board, from which he could then organize a demerger of the subsidiary Saatchi & Saatchi Worldwide — one of the options that had originally been reviewed and then rejected by Suzanna Taverne the previous year. When news of the proposal was made public a few days later, the industry was astounded. Almost everyone had assumed that Charles would quickly follow his brother into New Saatchi. But the plan was quickly rejected by the board. "How could we possibly have him back now, after the vitriolic media war between the two of us?" commented one of the company's directors anonymously in the *Financial Times*. It was easy to understand the disquiet felt by many at Charlotte Street. The company's share price appeared to be in terminal decline. From a price of 154 pence before Maurice's ousting, it had fallen to 109, then to 100, and finally bottomed out just above 80 before inching upwards again.

Charles himself learned of the board's decision not to cooperate from the newspapers. Nobody had bothered to contact him personally. But soon he was ready to try again. "Charles thought, OK, it's more important that there's a peace than the fact that someone had put his nose out of joint," says a close friend, "and about a month later he did try again." This time Charles said Maurice and his colleagues would agree not to take on any of the old company's clients or employees even if they wanted to join them for the next six months, in exchange for Saatchi & Saatchi dropping the lawsuits. Once again his efforts were rejected by the company.

Meanwhile there were fresh rumors in the press. The *Observer* speculated that Maurice might be teaming up with Tim Bell to seize back control. With no peace in sight, Maurice decided it was time to start hitting out at Oldco again. If they threatened to take him to court, he would countersue for breach of contract, he said. The agency retaliated by saying it intended to contest his claims "with vigor." A couple of days later Saatchi & Saatchi served Bill Muirhead with a writ accusing him of misappropriating confidential files and information belonging to the group and claiming damages of some $50 million. It was claimed, according to a newspaper report, that an elevator mechanic had spotted Muirhead removing boxes of files from the New York agency the weekend before his resignation. The company, it said, was claiming that these files had contained confidential details of how profitable individual clients' accounts were and how much Saatchi & Saatchi paid their key employees. Back in London, Muirhead was furious about the allegations. He knew he had gone through all the regulation security checks when entering and leaving the Hudson Street building that weekend after Christmas. He knew that the security video would be able to substantiate his claim to innocence. He was so incensed by this smear on his personal reputation — these people are calling me a liar and a thief, he told his two Sackville Street colleagues — that a few weeks later he would decide to bring suit for libel against the company, engaging the expertise of the well-known barrister George Carman to help him to fight the case.

By the third week of January the battle had become still

bloodier. Someone had tipped off the press about the details of the Saatchi brothers' extravagant expense accounts. Nonexecutive director Tom Russell, still bitter about the fortune the Saatchis had made from the Adidas deal, told the *Independent on Sunday*, "I think Maurice has a lot of explaining to do to the shareholders. On the compensation committee we saw expenses that we thought were not appropriate to the conduct of a public company and we moved to thwart them. There were some pretty serious excesses on the part of Maurice." Russell even said he recalled a shareholders meeting where elderly small investors had been stuffing sandwiches provided by the company into their pockets in what he claimed was the most vividly illustrated example of the consequences of financial mismanagement he had ever witnessed.

But then came a real bombshell for Saatchi & Saatchi. The *Sunday Times* ran a report claiming that directors of the company were facing a $150-million legal action from angry American investors, furious at the drop in the value of their shares. According to the report, lawyers in Los Angeles acting on behalf of an outfit called Arkhurst Investments and other investors had put the board on notice of their claim, which apparently alleged that the Saatchi board acted "negligently and without due care and diligence" in sacking Maurice Saatchi. "As a result of your negligent behavior, the share price has fallen by over 30 percent," they claimed, also reserving the right to seek exemplary damages from Charles Scott, the acting chairman.

Scott, meanwhile, was trying to contain the damage. The man described by Tim Bell as a "colorless bean-counter" attempted to play down the effects of Maurice's abrupt departure. The company's share price might have dropped by a third since Maurice sold his stake in early January, but its survival was definitely not under threat, he insisted. There were reports that Peter Davis, the former head of publishing giant Reed Elsevier, was being considered for the job of chairman of Saatchi & Saatchi PLC. The City seemed to approve and the speculation — for that was all it turned out to be — did the company no harm at all. Scott claimed to be no stranger to crisis and insisted that the current events were nothing like as catastrophic for the company as the mess he had had to deal with when he had been appointed financial director of Saatchi & Saatchi six years earlier. "Within twenty-four hours of agreeing to join in October 1989," he recalled, "I found the financial situation of the company made it virtually bankrupt. I spent the whole of Christmas negotiating with the banks to allow it to continue trading."

But even as he was attempting to reduce a difficult situation to a numbers game, more employees were being poached by Maurice. A Charlotte Street copywriter and art director from the British Airways team announced they were going to Davies Street, as did the head of the account at the agency, Tim Duffy. Then the *Sunday Times* announced that Harris Associates, the Chicago fund manager for which David Herro worked, was putting itself up for sale. Herro, one of thirteen partners in Harris, privately insisted that the sale was totally unconnected with the Saatchi & Saatchi fracas. Victor Morgenstern, the president of Harris, supported this claim, but did add that they considered the Saatchi affair an unfortunate episode. "In our own perspective we are passive investors, and we got a higher profile than we would like in Saatchi," he told the paper. "We regret the fact it got as messy as it did. Maurice Saatchi could have made a great contribution to the company and it was never our desire to see him leave." He went on, "David Herro made himself more accessible to the media than he should have. It's our policy not to get involved in management, which is why I say we have regrets. It has not been good for us, nor for the company, and we would be very reluctant to get involved in this way in the future. But Herro remains with us."

Events began to take a sinister turn: Sinclair, Kershaw, and Muirhead informed the police that friends and relatives of theirs had been getting phone calls from people claiming to be British Telecom workers checking numbers. BT denied involvement. The three believed that someone at Saatchi & Saatchi had been going through the records of their last phone calls from the office to see if they had been calling clients with a view to poaching them and thereby breaking their contracts. According to Kershaw, these reports triggered "an extraordinary paranoia" among the amigos, who suddenly began to notice white vans with no windows and big aerials parked outside their temporary office on Sackville Street. They also started spotting an unusually large number of people reading newspapers in their cars on the street below, "quite an innocent pastime, one would think, but these become figures of tremendous suspicion when you live under the influence of gardening paranoia," he said.

It was almost a relief when the two sides finally confronted one another in the High Court in early February. This was an initial hearing; the main case was still some months away and probably would not be heard until the summer. At the outset Saatchi & Saatchi appeared to have a strong case against David Kershaw, Bill Muirhead, and Jeremy Sinclair. Each had left without serving notice, amounting to a breach of their contracts, and had been put on gardening leave by the company. On February 8, the first day of the hearing, the three said they were happy to garden, as they called it, in the short term, but they knew in theory the company could try and stop them working for years, according to the terms of their individual contracts. They intended to fight this, they said, by claiming constructive dismissal on the grounds that Maurice Saatchi had been removed against their express advice. It was highly unlikely anyway that a court would enforce constraints for more than a year, but the three wanted to be free as soon as possible. They were hoping that they might be able to work at the new agency within as little as six months of walking out of Saatchi & Saatchi in such a dramatic fashion.

In their affidavits each tried to play down his individual ability to damage the business of the old company. Bill Muirhead said that he did not think he had any competitive advantage with the agency's clients above his personal friendships with some of them. He argued that, having been in the United States for almost a year, he had lost touch with the details of the U.K. business, and because he had been so involved in restructuring the U.S. company, he had met only some, not all, of that company's clients. David Kershaw claimed that he too did not know all the agency's clients personally. He pointed out, rather ironically, that clients rarely move for the sake of individuals. Jeremy Sinclair was in the strongest position because, as he said, as creative director of the company he had very little contact with clients at all. He asserted that he had not induced anyone to leave Saatchi & Saatchi and had done nothing to breach the terms of the restrictive covenants in his own contract that stopped him from working. In fact, all three had stuck assiduously to the conditions of their gardening leave, sitting in their Sackville Street office. They had been to visit Maurice at Davies Street, but nothing more. Their lawyers had told them that they could not do any real work for the new agency if they wanted to have any chance of winning the court case.

The company's case against Maurice was far shakier. By removing him as group chairman they had breached his service contract, which meant in effect they could not stop him from working elsewhere. It was on this basis that he had pushed ahead with the new agency, while actively recruiting people from Saatchi & Saatchi to join him. But the case was complicated by the company's claim that Maurice had attempted to damage its business and by its accusation that he had solicited the three amigos to join him in breach of their employment contracts. It took less than a week for Mr. Justice Jonathan Parker to rule in favor of Maurice. He even accused the company of attempting to stop Maurice establishing his new agency "by the back door," adding that now "the back door is firmly closed."

The ruling was a triumph for Maurice and the Sackville Three, especially as the judge said that Saatchi & Saatchi should pay all costs for this hearing, even if it won the case when it eventually came to court in the summer. David Kershaw was the only representative from the New Saatchi side in court. As he left, he told waiting reporters that the outcome was "terrific news," adding that he could not understand why Saatchi & Saatchi wanted to "strangle Maurice's company at birth." He asked, "If they thought he was so awful that they had to fire him, why don't they just let him compete?" Muirhead also had received good news from the States. A New York judge had ruled that he would not hear the $50-million case against him until the British proceedings were settled. The pressure, for the time being at least, was off.

Maurice was ecstatic. He told the press later that day that he intended to build the best agency in the world. The top position was still crucial to him, as he indicated when talking about the old company.

"If the agency does lose its place this year, it will be a tragedy," he said. "This is something my former colleagues now left at the agency never understood. They always said they didn't necessarily want to be the biggest agency at number one, but they wanted to be the most profitable. What they never grasped is that being the number one agency in this country was a passport onto pitch lists, because you are then too big and prominent to not make it onto a list for any serious piece of business which is moving."

He also sent a message to the management of Saatchi & Saatchi, telling them to give up the fight against him. "You can't put the toothpaste back in the tube," he said. "Clients have the right to choose." Maurice was once again the confident man of Saatchi & Saatchi's eighties heyday. He had long since thrown off his sackcloth and ashes. He had had his company stolen from him in the most ruthless manner and he was going to show them now what a mistake they had made.

"Make no mistake," said a former colleague at Saatchi & Saatchi, "all of this, every single move the company makes, is revenge. Revenge! Revenge! Revenge!"

Saatchi & Saatchi made a desperate attempt to limit the damage of the court decision by telling the press, "This was a skirmish in the war. It's not the war itself." One of its main objectives, keeping the three former executives "out of the market," had been achieved, it said. At Charlotte Street the new management put out a memo to its staff claiming that the decision was a victory because it had effectively stopped either David Kershaw, Bill Muirhead, or Jeremy Sinclair from working on the upcoming pitch for British Airways. "This is a very important result for us as it protects our business and people, irrespective of today's press headlines," it read. "The purpose of going to court is not to persecute the individuals but to safeguard our business from constant attack," it went on. "This has been achieved. We should all get on with the business of being brilliant, as this is the greatest asset we have."

The next day the company decided that there were actually more important things than just "being brilliant" after all, and attacked the former chairman yet again by seeking a further injunction to ban him from using his own name in the title of his new agency. "Names are registered by a company, not an individual," said a spokesman. "We want to make sure Maurice does not infringe our trademark and ensure that buyers in the marketplace do not have services passed off as those of Saatchi & Saatchi when in fact they are supplied by someone else."

The other side, fresh from celebrating their victory, could barely believe this latest twist. It seemed an extraordinary position to take. Maurice could hardly be stopped from using his own name, they thought. Calling the agency New Saatchi, besides being accurate of course, implied the original company was old and tired. David Kershaw spoke out. "You can't stop a person using their name. Perhaps the PLC will be accused of 'passing off' if their new name involves the word 'advertising.'"

A day later Saatchi & Saatchi confirmed that it had given the Stock Exchange details of confidential information allegedly passed by Maurice to a journalist. The company believed that this information, allegedly passed in January 1994 to Ivan Fallon, the Saatchi brothers' biographer and the former deputy editor of the *Sunday Times,* broke the Stock Exchange's strict rules. Maurice quickly replied that he had never actually sent the memo in question and Ivan Fallon said he had never received it. Saatchi's also gave the Stock Exchange details of a share transaction allegedly carried out on behalf of Maurice, which also might have broken the rules. The company was throwing as much at him as it could muster. It had finally realized that it was in the middle of all-out war.

The next offensive came almost immediately with the revelation that Saatchi & Saatchi intended to sue Charles and Maurice for up to $38 million, the amount believed to have been paid to the brothers and their private investment company as a result of their stake in Adidas. Maurice riposted that the company was "issuing writs like confetti" and added that he hoped they kept on issuing writs at such a pace because "a writ a day keeps the clients away." And then, in a reference to accounts like Mars and British Airways, he said: "If they paid as much attention to their clients as they do to their lawsuits, they might not have $500 million of business up for review."

As relations between Maurice Saatchi and the company he had founded with his brother continued to deteriorate, Charles still remained its official president. But when it finally emerged in court that he intended to join his brother in the new agency, the company brought an action against him to try and stop him from helping to set up an operation that, it claimed, would infringe Saatchi & Saatchi's trademark. Charles still had four years of a five-year contract to run, earning a salary of £312,500 a year. Apart from working on accounts like Gallaher, the tobacco company, and the Conservative Party during election time, his involvement with the company was now minimal. One of his friends reports, "Charles felt bad enough about what had happened to the company in the late eighties. Now he was telling everyone that what was happening was terrible, terrible." Eventually, in February, he submitted to the inevitable and handed in his resignation, pledging at the same time to sue the company for constructive dismissal on the grounds that life at the London agency had become intolerable. Once again the company hit out, claiming that he had released the news of his resignation to the press and the City before informing the agency itself. It dismissed any possibility of a payout to Charles just because he had so many years left to run on his contract. One insider told the *Financial Times*: "His resignation has saved everybody a lot of trouble. His position was becoming increasingly untenable."

The day the last Saatchi walked out of Saatchi & Saatchi was the end of an era for the company. There were doubtless some people who were glad, there might even have been a small celebration somewhere, but most of the staff were very sad to see him go. The final link with the past had been severed. Charles's decision to leave had followed the announcement a few days earlier that Gallaher had decided to switch its advertising for Silk Cut cigarettes to Maurice's new agency. Charles, who had originally conceived the campaign, was still contracted to work on the account at the express desire of Gallaher's management. A few days later Private Patients Plan, the medical insurance company, also said it was signing with Maurice in a deal worth some £4 million a year in billings. The company, in Britain second only to BUPA in medical insurance, had not used an advertising agency before, although it had worked with a Saatchi-group marketing company the previous year. Maurice was ebullient: "This is a milestone for both organizations," he said. "PPP is an ambitious, innovative company keen to make a difference in a burgeoning market."

At Charlotte Street, the people left behind were preparing to hold their Christmas party, delayed for two months after all the trauma. Based on a science-fiction theme, the party, held in a warehouse in King's Cross, was officially entitled "Star Trek, the Next Generation." The irony was not lost on those left behind after Maurice's and Charles's departures. There was indeed management by the next generation at Charlotte Street, but some felt the new team was so inexperienced it could have been from another planet altogether. The whole atmosphere of the company had changed in the space of just a few weeks. Once one of the most aggressive and successful agencies in town, it was now a place under siege, a place that spent more time filing suits against former employees than reassuring worried clients and producing campaigns. Many said privately that it was no fun working for Saatchi & Saatchi anymore. With both Saatchi brothers gone, people in the advertising industry were calling the company the Ampersand.

Campaign was still backing Maurice. "In the end, Maurice has rewritten the rules of the industry so many times that he clearly has the vision and motivation to tempt more clients away from the can-do-anything environment of Charlotte Street," it wrote. "And no one should forget that setting up new agencies and pirating key staff is, after all, business as usual for the ad industry."

eleven   DisCordiant

*T*HE OLD SAATCHI finally bowed to David Herro's long-time demand. On March 16, 1995, at an extraordinary general meeting held in the City of London, investors were asked to approve the holding company's change of name. As the lights dimmed and the sounds of a medieval Gregorian chant filled the hall, a giant sign hanging over the podium began to unfold, revealing the legend in big black letters. Henceforth Saatchi & Saatchi PLC would be known as Cordiant — a title selected, according to a letter to shareholders, "as an expression of the new spirit within the company, characterized by accord and shared purpose."

Shareholders who had voted in favor of a name change were delighted. Others were less pleased, or just embarrassed by the ceremony. Even some of Maurice's opponents had to admit that the new name was second-rate — but exactly what you'd expect from a company that had lost its "creative" figureheads. One speaker thought Cordiant sounded more like a vacuum-cleaner business, or a new kind of soft drink, than an advertising agency. Others suggested that DisCordiant, or perhaps Cormorant, would have been a more appropriate title. The name Cordiant was the creation of Siegel & Gale, a U.S.-based corporate identity company and a subsidiary of Saatchi & Saatchi. Derived from the Latin for "heart," they said, the name "expresses a core or heart position" that the holding company has at "the center of one of the world's leading communications groups."

At last, here was an opportunity for the ordinary investors, who had been unable to do anything but watch helplessly as the value of their holdings fell in the preceding weeks, to confront the board about the ousting of Maurice Saatchi. Ronald Moss began the proceedings by demanding that the directors indicate with a show of hands how many of them had supported the move to oust Maurice Saatchi. They refused. He then asked the nonexecutives to list how many other directorships they held, demanding to know how much time these other commitments left them to devote to Saatchi & Saatchi business. Another shareholder argued that lawyers should not be allowed to gobble up millions of pounds for legal actions against former employees. The number of lawsuits was ridiculous and made the company look absurd, he said. Catherine Simmonds, a former employee and now a shareholder, paraphrased Oscar Wilde: "To lose one Saatchi brother may be a misfortune, to lose two looks like carelessness." She criticized the "bizarre actions" of the board, pouring scorn on the new name.

The meeting was at least as uncomfortable as the board had expected, but the fact still remained that the company was free of Maurice Saatchi. And if Cordiant was intended to express a new spirit of "accord and shared purpose" within the company, the views of a few overzealous small investors could easily be ignored in the interests of greater harmony.

After so much bad publicity, Charles Scott was craving

anonymity. Only days before the EGM, he had had to tell the City that yet again the company, which had been on the road to recovery until last December, would be unable to pay out any dividends. "Inevitably, the turmoil will affect our performance in 1995," he said. "Instead of being a year of continuing recovery, it will be a year of transition." Scott had long envied Martin Sorrell, the former financial director of Saatchi & Saatchi, who was now running Ogilvy & Mather and J. Walter Thompson from the relative safety of a holding company called WPP. When Sorrell's company was in financial trouble, it was always reported as the plight of WPP and rarely reflected on the advertising agencies themselves, which were able to preserve their good names and continue trading normally.

On the day of the EGM, Charles Scott was still trying to recover from the crushing blow dealt to the company by Mars two weeks before. Mars had finally decided to pull its entire advertising account, worth $400 million worldwide, out of all the Bates agencies. Those who had hoped the Mars brothers were only bluffing when they had warned the company of the consequences of sacking Maurice Saatchi now knew they had made a serious error. The account had brought in £30 million a year in revenue — equivalent to Cordiant's entire profit for 1994. The day the announcement had been made, the company's share price took another tumble, from 105 pence to 94.5 pence. The Mars decision was one of the biggest account moves in the history of advertising. The only consolation was that Mars had not gone straight to Maurice's new agency but had instead transferred its business to a number of Cordiant's multinational rivals. There was speculation that hundreds of jobs would have to go, though Scott insisted that the agency would be hanging on to all but a handful of the people who had worked on the account, to help it pitch for other business. Yet everyone knew that Mars was the glue that held Bates together internationally; without it the future looked even more uncertain. Wendy Smyth, the acting chief operating officer of Saatchi & Saatchi PLC, told the *Times,* "We didn't actually believe they would've taken all the business away."

A few days before the EGM, however, the holding company discovered that it had some good news to announce at last. As a result of a very careful search, it had finally found a new chairman, not to replace Maurice Saatchi as head of Saatchi & Saatchi PLC but to replace David Kershaw as head of the London agency.

Jennifer Laing had joined Compton in 1969 as a graduate trainee and had worked for the company off and on during her career. Tim Bell had tempted her back to Charlotte Street in the eighties with the promise of a red Ferrari — the ultimate yuppie status symbol. In March 1995 she was wooed back from her own small agency, Laing Henry, by a salary of £175,000 and a Toyota sedan (Toyota being one of Saatchi & Saatchi's less Maurice-friendly accounts). "Oh, the Ferrari was just a symbol," Laing remarks, "an assertive, conspicuous symbol of success. Totally inappropriate to life in the nineties. Awful really." Laing was always eager to play down the effects of Maurice's departure on the London agency, echoing Scott's insistent defense. "Only eleven people have left Charlotte Street. There are six hundred left. It was not exactly a mass exodus. Saatchi's is still number one in the U.K., with around a hundred good clients and £465 million worth of billings. That doesn't sound to me like a company going out of business," she insisted. She caused great amusement with her promise to wrap her arms around the remaining clients at the agency to reassure them they were in capable hands.

There were rumors that other clients had threatened to walk out unless the agency cut its rates. The new management tried to remain firm and a spokesman insisted the agency was "not rolling over and accepting business at any cost," adding, "We had a new client that wanted certain terms which were flatly rejected." No names, of course, were mentioned. Only one big client had made a point of expressing its loyalty to Saatchi & Saatchi and Cordiant. Procter & Gamble had awarded the company a new assignment with billings of an estimated £25 million.

Maurice was still besieging the agency by phone, trying to recruit the best people by offering them raises of at least 10 percent. It felt like a talent contest. Those who were proud to have been contacted in the very early days, ahead of their less fortunate colleagues, were soon crestfallen when they realized he was calling virtually the entire agency in roughly alphabetical order. Loyalties were divided, and one anonymous Saatchi staffer spoke for many when she told *Campaign*: "Everyone who works at Charlotte Street learned their trade from someone who learned from someone who learned from someone who learned from Maurice or Charles or Bill [Muirhead] or Jeremy [Sinclair]. The spirit that they've passed on is so inspirational that people like me, who weren't even born twenty-five years ago, habitually invoke it every day and feel the need to keep it alive. I just don't know whether the best way to keep it alive is to go or to stay."

New Saatchi was continuing to poach old Saatchi clients, finally in April going after one of the most prestigious accounts in the world, British Airways. Old Saatchi had handled BA's advertising since 1982 and the account alone was worth more to it than the size of its £60-million budget. To many at Charlotte Street, the globe-beating airline had come to symbolize so many of the agency's own qualities: its international successes, its eighties boom, its very heart and culture. But anyone who knew anything about Maurice's relationship with BA's president, Lord King, and its chairman, Sir Colin Marshall, knew the agency had a shaky hold on the account without him.

Four agencies had been short-listed to compete for a year-long contract: Saatchi & Saatchi, New Saatchi, J. Walter Thompson, and Bartle Bogle Hegarty. JWT, part of Martin Sorrell's WPP empire, was still considered one of the old masters of advertising. It was a big, solid, reputable giant of an agency with offices around the world and a London base on Berkeley Square. Bartle Bogle Hegarty could not have been more different. Still run by its three founding partners, John Bartle, Nigel Bogle, and John Hegarty, it was a young agency with offices in the heart of Soho, producing sexy, award-winning campaigns for clients such as Levi's and Häagen-Dazs. Each agency had been allotted a day to make initial presentations and had been briefed carefully by the BA team. It was clear from the outset that the airline was interested in ideas on the future direction of its advertising campaigns and on the logistics of handling such a big account in all the major countries of the world. The winning agency would beat the others by having the best overall strategy for BA's communications, rather than the best idea for a wacky new ad.

JWT had been waiting for the chance to get its hands on the BA account for as long as most people in the industry could remember. It had been preparing itself for the chance to pitch for at least five years. On the first Monday morning in April, Dominic Proctor, the affable young chief executive, was waiting nervously in his office for the arrival of the BA team, led in the first round by Derek Dear, the company's general manager for marketing communications and a loyal employee for almost thirty years. The agency had been told it would be the first of the four to give its presentation, and it was desperate to make a good impression. Members of JWT's pitch team had spent the last few weeks flying around the world courtesy of BA, visiting different offices and talking to regional directors. JWT was nothing if not conscientious. By the morning of the pitch, every detail had been carefully considered, right down to the staff in reception, who had all been decked out in T-shirts bearing the words BA GROUND SUPPORT STAFF.

No one at BA seriously expected any of the agencies to use the whole day it had been allotted. But by four in the afternoon the BA officials were still at JWT, going through a series of long and extremely thorough presentations. The agency had concentrated on the strength of its worldwide network of offices. It knew that neither BBH nor New Saatchi could hope to compete with all its resources. But JWT had not done as well as it had hoped. Almost immediately there were rumors that the airline's executives had looked around the vast complex of offices and muttered the ominous words "death by overhead" to one another.

Maurice Saatchi's presentation could not have been more different. Because the amigos were still on gardening leave, he had been forced to put the presentation together himself with the help of Tim Duffy, who had formally been in charge of the account at Saatchi & Saatchi before joining Maurice's new enterprise earlier in the year. Working out of the tiny Davies Street offices, Maurice had none of the teams of people so readily at the disposal of JWT. With no one else to send up to BA headquarters near Heathrow, he had made several visits himself, touring the purchasing department, talking to the local managers. This was the great adman himself getting to grips with the nuts and bolts of the business, much to the amusement of some in the marketing department, who were more accustomed to seeing him schmoozing with their bosses than touring the shop floor. Here was the perfect opportunity for Maurice to reinvent himself as the very model of a hard-working adman. He was in his element.

Maurice had been aware from the start that he could not possibly conduct the presentation at Davies Street. He needed a more impressive arena to remind the world's favorite airline of the Saatchi pizazz — the glamour, the glitz, the excitement of working with the Saatchis. At the time the agency was close to signing a deal on larger offices on Kingly Street, just behind Regent Street. They had already outgrown Davies Street, with the creative department now working in a room next door above a firm of real-estate agents, while others had moved into a temporary office in Islington. Maurice charmed the Kingly Street landlord into allowing him to use the building for their BA presentation. It was just like the old days at Golden Square, although this time Charles did not need to go out onto the street and pay people to come in for half an hour and look busy. A special reception area and board-room were build for the occasion. Maurice wanted BA to know he was on his way up again. The message was, Saatchi & Saatchi without the Saatchis just would never be the same.

He was still facing one other rather large problem, however. Having sold the concept of globalization to BA so convincingly in the eighties, Maurice Saatchi now had to convince them that his new operation could manage their advertising all around the world — a seemingly impossible task for an agency only three months old, with only forty people and no offices outside London. He had been negotiating for some time with different large international advertising companies to find one that he could tie up with to handle the BA account. Finally, at the beginning of the week in which the first round of presentations were due to take place, Maurice was able to announce a deal. He had decided to sign with Publicis, the Paris-based giant founded by the legendary Marcel Bleustein-Blanchet, which would give New Saatchi access to 180 offices in fifty-six countries and 7,000 people. The chairman of Publicis Communication, another Maurice, Maurice Lévy, flew in for the presentation to BA.

Derek Dear was dazzled by the prospect of Maurice Saatchi leading the pitch to win back an account his former agency had held since 1982. It was strange to be receiving so much personal attention from the adman who mixed with the stars and who had long since risen above the nitty-gritty of the everyday management of advertising accounts. Over the years the relationship between the airline and Saatchi & Saatchi had not always been smooth. In 1992 there had been a major crisis when the production costs of one of BA's big international commercials had gone thousands of pounds over budget. The agency had fallen out with the commercial's director, Tony Kaye, after an argument over whether or not it had approved the additional costs. The battle had dragged on for years and the dispute was only finally settled in April 1995, just before the outcome of the pitches was announced. The whole affair had become particularly embarrassing for BA when Kaye started publicly accusing the company of racism in its choice of people to star in the commercial. He had even held a demonstration outside BA's offices with a hundred actors dressed up to look like Hasidic Jews, complete with hats and beards and carrying placards.

But Dear had been looking forward to Maurice Saatchi's

presentation. After three days of leading the team around the other agencies, he had had enough of long, worthy presentations, endless discussions of resources and international networks. He was longing for something livelier and he knew Maurice could always be relied on to produce theater, to bring a bit of the showbiz back to advertising. He was not disappointed. As Maurice greeted BA in Kingly Street's temporary reception and they walked towards the elevator, something caught Dear's eye. Just for a split second he thought he saw Bill Muirhead, Jeremy Sinclair, and David Kershaw standing over on the other side of the room waving at him. He could not help but smile when he realized that he had actually seen three life-sized cardboard cutouts of the three amigos still on gardening leave, an apt reminder of all the legal action initiated by the old company.

BBH had been caught by surprise when they were told they were on the shortlist for the BA account. Like Maurice, they had no international network of advertising agencies, though they too were confident they could find a suitable partner, and also like Maurice they could not match the resources of either JWT or Saatchi & Saatchi. They knew they had done well in the first round of presentations. The idea of leaving the BA people to have lunch with some of their most loyal clients had been very well received. "They thought it was great to meet other clients and they enjoyed talking about marketing over lunch, sharing problems and experiences," says Hegarty. "We literally had to drag them away at three o'clock to continue our presentation." BA had liked the young, creative atmosphere of BBH. Within days of the end of the first round, Derek Dear was on the phone asking more questions — a good sign, John Hegarty knew. He and his two partners could barely believe their good fortune.

Meanwhile at Charlotte Street there was a depressed atmosphere. Ed Wax, who had flown over from New York especially for the pitch, knew that many people at the agency were convinced BA had already decided to move its account elsewhere. But Saatchi & Saatchi had begun the pitch on a high note, having just launched their latest commercial for the airline a few days before the first round of presentations. Everyone had loved the big-budget ad, directed by Hugh Hudson; the opening shots of helicopters flying towards an island that was later covered in red, white, and blue silk had made a favorable impression on critics in the industry. It was global advertising on a grand scale and no one outside the agency seemed to realize that the entire commercial had been orchestrated by people who had subsequently left the company to join up with Maurice. But the staff at Saatchi & Saatchi knew the truth and despondency had set in, exacerbated by rumors that the real competition for the account was between New Saatchi and BBH.

It was Maurice's close friend Sir Colin Marshall who led the team back to Saatchi & Saatchi at the beginning of the second round of visits to the four agencies. On this occasion each company would have just two hours to argue its case. The presentation at Charlotte Street did not go well. JWT, however, did much better the second time around. Its people seemed to have relaxed since the first occasion and their presentation was snappy and to the point. "They cut out all the crap and just gave us the good stuff," said one senior BA executive afterwards. Maurice and his team had been working on their two-hour presentation nonstop. This time he wanted to really show them that New Saatchi meant serious business. Spiriting the BA team back up to the boardroom in Kingly Street, he showed them a specially prepared interview with Sir Andrew Lloyd Webber, who had offered to write the music for BA's next commercial. He had never been involved in advertising before, he said, but Maurice had persuaded him it could be interesting. Then came a film starring the actor John Cleese, and another with Sir John Egan, chief executive of the British Airports Authority. But the best came last — a personal message from the media baron Rupert Murdoch himself, talking about the kinds of deals BA might be able to negotiate through New Saatchi, as part of a massive advertising campaign in his worldwide chain of newspapers and television channels. It was an impressive two hours, even in Maurice Saatchi's terms.

The BA team had told all the advertising agencies that they would reach their final decision in a couple of days, certainly before the weekend. But when Friday arrived they said they needed a few more days to make up their minds. There were rumors that BA was split, with Derek Dear and his team favoring BBH and Sir Colin Marshall favoring his old friend Maurice. It was agony for the four competitors. Maurice headed for Old Hall in Sussex for the weekend. Allen Thomas, JWT's worldwide creative director, went fishing in Wiltshire. John Hegarty went home to Highgate in north London. "I couldn't sleep really at all and when I did I was dreaming one minute that we had won it and the next that we had lost," he says. Bill Muirhead, feeling helpless in the Sackville potting shed, spent the long weekend walking around in a T-shirt with the words "Losing is not an option" emblazoned across the front. He insisted he was in such agony that he could not bring himself either to wash or to shave until BA had made up their minds.

On Monday morning Maurice Saatchi got a call from BA asking him to come over to their corporate offices on Berkeley Square.

As soon as he left the building, the small staff at New Saatchi gave up any pretense of working. They sat around in small groups talking quietly. Muirhead, Kershaw, and Sinclair came over from Sackville Street, impatient to hear what was happening. Maurice returned less than an hour later and asked everyone to gather around. He had some news, he said. He told them that he had been to see BA. He told them that BA had made what they described as a very difficult decision. He said in the end it had been a very close contest. And then he told them. Yes, they had won the account. There was a huge cheer. Muirhead felt faint with relief, Kershaw fought to stop the tears welling up in his eyes.

King and his team had been seduced by the Saatchi showmanship — the showmanship and the seeming ability to make anything possible. "We have always looked to our advertising agency to give us an exciting view of life," said Dear afterwards. "We would like to think that the airline and travel business are glamorous. We were looking for an agency which would be bold enough to come to us with big, wacky ideas. Of course we might reject a lot of them, but I would prefer that every time to an agency which is just not creative enough, which offers work that simply won't inspire our consumers, that won't make a difference. This was at the heart of our decision and it was Maurice's team that had the big ideas, big ideas in abundance."

In his new spirit, as head of his new family, Maurice asked the entire new agency down to his Sussex mansion the following weekend for a party. As he turned over the sausages on the barbecue himself and handed around the rolls, rarely had so many people felt so honored.

Meanwhile Ed Wax, at old Saatchi, told the *New York Times,* "We believe this is the last shoe to drop." But more bad news was literally days away. Later that week, the electrical retailer Dixons confirmed that it was indeed moving its £40-million account to Maurice's new agency, affecting between fifty and eighty jobs at Saatchi's, since it was one of the most labor-intensive accounts the agency held. The next day, however, Charlotte Street announced it had won an account at last — after losing so many. Comet was coming in to replace Dixons, and although its business was worth much less, with an average annual advertising budget of just £24 million a year, the news was a welcome relief. The following week the company told the world in the best way it could that it was still fighting. In a double-page advertisement in the *Times,* it asked: "So, who wants to be the world's favorite now?"

The company was still facing the High Court hearing against Maurice and the amigos, now scheduled for June, the same month as its annual general meeting. Charles Scott had already tried to answer questions from shareholders about the mounting legal bills at the EGM in March and he had no desire to face them again in the summer. The company was ready to settle. It had stopped three of its former senior executives from working for six months and from taking part in the BA pitch for New Saatchi. Maurice also had no desire to go to court. He was trying to establish his new agency, he had a lot of new clients, he needed to find new offices (the agreement on Kingly Street had fallen through — ironically, they had lost the building to one of their opponents for the BA account, Bartle Bogle Hegarty). The lawyers for both sides started talking.

With a settlement in sight, one last problem emerged. Charles and Maurice managed to obtain a copy of potentially damaging notes in Cordiant's 1994 annual report, still being prepared, on their pension entitlements in 1989. The notes suggested that £2.9

million that was transferred out of the Saatchi & Saatchi Pension and Assurance plan in 1989 to the brothers' private plan, after Charles and Maurice had been members of it for just a year, might have been "calculated incorrectly." The brothers immediately sought legal advice to see if they could get an injunction to prevent publication of the report unless Cordiant agreed to delete the offending paragraph.

The lawyers continued to talk and four weeks later the two sides finally settled out of court. The agreement seemed like complete capitulation on the part of Cordiant. The Saatchi brothers established they could use their family name in the title of the new company, which it was agreed, at least in the short term, would be called M&C Saatchi (soon nicknamed McSaatchi); they could keep all the staff they had poached from the old company, although they agreed not to take any more that year; Bill Muirhead, Jeremy Sinclair, and David Kershaw were free to stop gardening and start working, although they would not receive the bonuses due to them from the old company; Cordiant agreed to drop its $50-million lawsuit against Muirhead in New York and apologized to him; it also agreed to meet the brothers' legal costs, estimated to be up to £250,000, plus its own legal fees; and it said it would drop the investigation into the pension fund, as well as abandoning any legal action over the Saatchis' investment in Adidas.

In the eyes of the world Cordiant had signed an unconditional surrender. The press release issued jointly by both sides stated that neither party would be making any further public announcements. The statement, curt and to the point, claimed that "representatives from both companies expressed satisfaction at the outcome." Indeed, Cordiant had actually gained what it considered to be a major victory. It had stopped Maurice calling his company New Saatchi: it hated the name New Saatchi, with the implication that it was the old company, outdated and with no future.

The annual general meeting in June was a subdued affair after the excitement of the EGM in March. Charles Scott said he now intended to draw a line under the last six months of the company's history and look to the future. He had summarized his thoughts in the annual report. "The past year has been a turbulent one," he wrote. "The culmination of this was marked in January 1995 by the departure of two of the directors of your company, Maurice Saatchi and Jeremy Sinclair. As with any period of upheaval, some things come to an end and many fresh starts are made. It is my duty as your Company's chief executive and acting chairman to guide the Company through this period of change and build the foundations of a stronger organization. The change of the Company's name to Cordiant marks a watershed; a change to a more professionally run group, built on a properly balanced partnership between clients, staff and shareholders."

Kevin McCormack, editor of *ADWEEK,* expressed his reservations about the new Saatchi agency, just as he had expressed them before about the old company under the Saatchi brothers: "While we wish the best for any start-up agency, in this case our concerns have to be less for the renegade gang, and more for the 10,990 people they left behind. And their clients."

The "renegades" soon to reemerge in the shape of M&C Saatchi were forced pretty quickly into setting up an operation in America by their new client British Airways. By the middle of 1996 they were claiming that their U.S. business accounted for around 20 percent of the company's total billings, with five clients — British Airways, Qantas, Hewlett Packard, Head, and Alamo. With an office of fifteen people, the company was laying plans to move into a new building on 42nd Street, the Daily News building featured in the *Superman* movies. There were also definite plans to open an office in Los Angeles, the agency hoping to have between fifty and sixty people working for the company in the U.S. by the end of the year. "We are planning to grow quickly, though not by acquisition this time," says Muirhead. Indeed, the agency is reported to have had talks with a number of agency groups about possible affiliations in the U.S. to help grow its market share. "We have to recognize that America is an important market for any serious advertising agency and it's critical to us," says Muirhead. "It's home to nearly three-quarters of the world's advertisers and we need to have a strong presence there. I didn't come to M&C to run a London boutique."

M&C Saatchi's performance in the U.K. in the year following the out-of-court settlement with Cordiant has been steady, if not as spectacular as the first few months of its existence. Clients like Courage Brewing and the ITV television network kept the agency growing to such an extent that it was planning in June 1996 to move into new offices in Golden Square — the site of the Saatchi & Saatchi's first offices in 1970 — before the end of the year. Mars's decision to award M&C Saatchi a £10 million project was hailed as a major victory by Maurice, and the agency's first work for the Conservative Party in May 1996 added some glamour — an essential Saatchi ingredient — to the agency's reputation.

Despite Bill Muirhead's protestations, the company has been slower getting off the ground in the U.S. Charles Scott commented in an interview in early 1996: "You can't expect us all to sit here and seriously see M&C Saatchi as the same type of threat as J. Walter Thompson, McCann Erickson, or BBDO. They're obviously a serious competitor in the United Kingdom, but they're not in the same league outside the United Kingdom." The *New York Times,* in February 1996, made a similar point: "Making a big splash in London, where the Saatchi mystique still runs strong, is one thing. Creating a presence and winning business in the intensely competitive and more risk-averse advertising climate of the United States is quite another, even for an agency of M&C Saatchi's pedigree." Nevertheless, in June 1996, the *New York Times* was reporting on the controversy generated by an M&C Saatchi campaign for British Airways developed in the New York office, sounding a familiar chord when noting that "the ads are certainly different from a lot of airline advertising."

Going back to their roots, as a fast-growing advertising agency still in its first year, seems to be suiting all the partners at M&C Saatchi. While Bill Muirhead is jetting around the world to establish regional bases, David Kershaw reports: "Maurice is turbocharged, he really enjoys every moment, all the young people, all the energy." And he will probably need all the energy he can muster, for now that the initial excitement is over he will need to steel himself for the everyday grind of building up a company from scratch. Maurice himself is optimistic: "We have been very fortunate," he says. "With the kind of accounts we already have, this has been a fairy-tale start for the company." *Campaign,* in its yearly agency report published in March 1996, gave M&C Saatchi nine points out of a possible ten, explaining that it has "proved to be far more than an empty monument to Maurice Saatchi's revenge on his former agency."

The company that Bill Muirhead and his cohorts left behind

in 1995 is equally bullish about the future. Having recruited former McCann-Erickson chief Bob Seleert as Saatchi & Saatchi Worldwide's president and chief operating officer, the company can see only growth ahead. The survival of Saatchi & Saatchi may never have been seriously in doubt, but now it seems the two Saatchi agencies are planning to coexist in the U.K., the U.S., and other major markets around the world, at least in the foreseeable future. Perhaps Maurice was right in the end. Nothing is impossible after all.

twelve STICK TO YOUR KNITTING

*I*N A WAY WHAT HAS HAPPENED to Maurice Saatchi is all
about what has happened to shareholder activism in recent years,
although that seems odd when you meet David Herro, because at
first sight the Chicago fund holder is a man of no obvious conse-
quence at all. To a lot of people, what he brought about at Saatchi
& Saatchi PLC was a disaster. If nothing else, the Saatchi im-
broglio has proved the old adage that in "creative" businesses such
as advertising, the most important assets the shareholders "own"
are people. They are the repositories of creativity, reputations, and
contacts, and if they are antagonized they can walk out the door,
taking much of the business with them.

One way to put in context the degree to which shareholder activism has worked its way into the culture at large is to consider
the kinds of allegations that have been made — almost casually —
in the last year or so against figures like Maurice Saatchi, not only
in the world of advertising but in the film industry too. In early
1995 Matsushita gave up on MCA, selling the Hollywood studio
whose elderly chairman, Lew Wasserman, it had found increasingly unbiddable. A month or so later, S. G. Warburg, a British

merchant bank, sold itself in a hurry to Swiss Bank Corporation, partly because so many of its people were quitting that its value was rapidly falling. David Herro, in his own inconsequential fashion, represents the confluence of all this.

In the six months after the Saatchi & Saatchi board voted to replace Maurice Saatchi as chairman, a decision that many observers at the time hailed as a victory for shareholders' rights began to look increasingly pyrrhic. Herro, of course, disagrees. He still declares that he has no regrets over the costly removal of the chairman. "Cordiant," he says, "will be a lot better off in the future." Unmoved by the short-term defection of so many clients and the dented morale of people working in London, he suggests that, from now on, "there will be unencumbered management decisions — that is, the management of the holding company is now free to manage, without having to worry about internal struggles and internal fighting and internal politics." In other words, he argues, the long-term effects on Cordiant's future will be minimal. "The company has maintained 95 percent of its revenues," he explains. "In the grand scheme of things, I think quite clearly it is a correct assessment that most of the business has stayed intact."

Herro has a point. Although the Mars decision was a blow, other large clients, including Procter & Gamble, have remained loyal. Given Maurice's long association with Lord King, it was always unlikely that British Airways would stay at Saatchi & Saatchi without him. The company did not destroy itself by sacking the chairman. But neither will it ever be the same again. Perhaps, with the departure of the brothers, Cordiant has lost something more important than just a name: it has lost the Saatchi Factor, the "virus," the outsiders' mentality of its two founders, who always believed that there were no unbreakable rules, that only success breeds success. "Saatchi's was like a mass psychosis," recalls a former employee. "When people joined they changed. They became convinced they were bigger and tougher. It was almost like a cult." It is therefore ironic to note that the same attitudes, the same philosophy — "Nothing is Impossible" — that led to Charles's and Maurice's rapid ascent in the world of international commerce also led to their sudden downfall. To some extent the Saatchi brothers rose to prominence on the London advertising scene by importing American practices. Ultimately, in Fitzrovia, on December 16, 1994, they fell from grace owing to a different kind of American export — the shareholder activist. "The self-interest of the brothers was the guiding force that made Saatchi's big in the first place," a former colleague observes. "They only stopped identifying with the agency when it stopped making progress. That's when their self-interest became separated."

The irony did not escape David Herro. "You know," he says, "in his resignation letter Maurice wrote, 'We've been taken over.' Well, we were the ones who had invested in the company when it was about to fall apart. The point wasn't that the brothers spent frivolously, and so on and so forth. The point, at least from a shareholder's perspective, is that a chairman of the board's job is to make sure that the shareholders' interests are represented in the management of the company."

It is probably not surprising that the new management of Cordiant continue to praise what he did. For them, too, the real problem was that Maurice could never accept that he had sold the company. "Public companies are owned by the people who have stock," Herro explains. "We elect Maurice Saatchi to chair a board to represent our interests. What was he doing ignoring our interests and putting his before ours? And to other owners of the company that is inappropriate behavior for a chairman. Maurice's use of those letters [from Forrest Mars and Sir Colin Marshall] was a form of extortion. He was saying, 'OK, if you guys are going to do that, I'm going to trash the company.' So does that give him permission to do anything he wants?"

During the heady days of early 1995, when Maurice was in the process of setting up the new agency, his primary motivation seemed to be revenge. The only accounts that M&C Saatchi won were those previously held by his old company. Inevitably, each victory for the Saatchi brothers was regarded as a defeat for Cordiant. Now Maurice has to prove that the new agency is also capable of winning business from J. Walter Thompson, Ogilvy & Mather, Bartle Bogle Hegarty, and others. "Even to get on a pitch for a non-Saatchi's client would indicate that here is an agency that has something new to offer," observed *Campaign* in May 1995. "By its very nature, revenge is something which burns itself out and if it is not underpinned or replaced by something more positive, then it is of questionable value when normal life resumes."

The first time I saw Maurice Saatchi after the boardroom upheaval, he was still in the process of moving into the Dress Rehearsal offices on Davies Street. He had cast himself in a new, unfamiliar role, and it was taking a bit of getting used to. One moment the chairman of a big famous public company, the next a part owner in a medium-sized London advertising agency with only a handful of offices around the world and one or two big accounts. The war between him and the old company was still raging in the press. In conversation with him over several days, I occasionally got the impression that he was saying and doing things for effect. He was charming, but still puzzled by the events of the past year. Sometimes he appeared to be Maurice Saatchi playing Maurice Saatchi. He could be volatile and unfair; more often he was frank, modest, insightful, and sensitive. For a while, he seemed to be torn between a desire to tell the real story of the Saatchi & Saatchi affair and a combination of anger and bitterness towards Herro. "I have learned that there are some very extraordinary people in this world," he said. "I'm not sure I could have done anything to prevent the situation, because David Herro had decided he wanted control of the company."

David Puttnam believes that Maurice Saatchi has the determination and single-mindedness to make a success of the new agency. "I think he can taste it, I really do," he says. But Maurice Saatchi's story is more complicated than that of someone trying to have a second chance for success. According to Cecil Parkinson, the younger Saatchi brother exudes a sort of magnetism. "Maurice looks very jovial and cheerful and approachable," he says, "but he's quite a toughie — very pleasant and civilized, but he's quite cold-eyed — and not a man to cross, as Cordiant has found out." Robert Louis-Dreyfus agrees that the deposed chairman of Saatchi & Saatchi PLC has an unusual robustness that will stand him in good stead in the future. "One of Maurice's great qualities," the Frenchman adds, "is that he is a street fighter, a ruthless street fighter." It may be that his fear is stronger than the passion he says he has for advertising. In fact, he may not be ready to get down to work again. He may be terrified that he will be terribly disappointed when it comes down to just plain old routine. He may be afraid that the world will be disappointed by his new agency. "The question is," says John Hegarty, "does a certain fire go out of the belly? It depends on how hungry Maurice and Charles are — and only they will know that for sure. The ones who compromise don't really succeed. They have had a fantastic start, and that will go on for another eighteen months at least, but what will it be like in five years' time?"

To some extent, of course, the unknown quantity in the equation is Charles and his preparedness or otherwise to put a shoulder to the wheel at the new agency. Depending on whom you talk to, Charles Saatchi in his heyday — the sixties and seventies — was a copywriting genius or a glib opportunist. He continues to provoke fierce loyalties. Take Paul Arden, for example, one of the most respected directors in today's advertising industry, who has this to say about Charles Saatchi: "What I find extraordinary to this day is his vision and maturity at such a young age. For me, in the end, the question is still: 'But what does Charlie think?'" Those who remember Maurice do so with much less affection. "He has a much colder personality than his brother," says one person who worked for the agency for many years. "I really wouldn't want anything to do with him now, but Charles, well, I still feel a lot of affection for Charles Saatchi."

Having made a personal fortune out of his contemporary art collection, Charles has no desire to become involved with the new agency's management. The man whose vision, energy, and enthusiasm had driven Saatchi & Saatchi forward at such a relentless pace over a quarter of a century has no desire to do it all again. "I'm not as involved as the others," he admits. "I think I'd like to take an interest but I don't want to get back into running the business in a full-time role. Obviously I'm very emotionally involved in it, but I enjoy my life and I don't want to get into an endless chase for bigger and better."

It is significant, perhaps, that Charles has discovered a new passion, karting, which he now approaches with the same single-mindedness that helped him build the Saatchi empire. He has become a karting fanatic. The sport is usually carried out on unheard-of race tracks in unglamorous parts of the Home Counties. As a rule, it attracts people who are more likely to roll up on a Sunday afternoon in a Ford Transit than a Bentley or Rolls-Royce. But Charles is no ordinary go-karter. He is in a different league from the other regular race-goers, with his two full-time mechanics, a truck for transporting his equipment to meets, the use of the Ricard workshop, where his engines are rebuilt, and a warehouse in Milton Keynes for all his spare parts. Charles Saatchi is no weekend driver; he likes to practice from Wednesday to Friday and occasionally on Tuesdays too. He even pays people to drive against him, so that he can polish up his technique.

In his spare time he will continue to work on the campaigns that particularly interest him, like Silk Cut and the Conservative Party, if it decides to move its account away from Saatchi & Saatchi before the next general election. Of course, in the wider context, as a fan, Charles still keeps abreast of developments in the world of advertising. In July 1995 his Saatchi Gallery in northwest London hosted an exhibition organized by Design and Art Direction that was originally going to be called "But Is It Art?" For several weeks in midsummer a space that has shown some of the most significant artists of the second half of the century, from Donald Judd and Richard Serra to Andy Warhol, became a temporary home to the full-size ninety-six-sheet advertising billboard version of Nike's poster featuring French soccer hero Eric Cantona. Other installations were devoted to the pioneering and much-celebrated work of director Tony Kaye, whose sepia-tinted feel-good films used chess players and children to promote British Rail.

In recent years there has been a marked stepping up of the

advertiser's traditional reliance on appeals to irrationality. This seems to be due at least in part to the nature of the television medium itself, where the director's multiple resources for influencing mood and atmosphere make it far easier to sidestep the skeptical reaction and exploit to the full the power of unconscious and semiconscious association. Abbott Mead Vickers's Dunlop commercial, for example, failed to explain what throwing a piano off the edge of a road really had to do with buying tires. A former adman, Tony Brignall, writing in *Campaign* earlier this year, focused his criticism on Tony Kaye, who directed the Dunlop commercial. "Far less excusable," he wrote, "is the belief creeping into his work and that of young people who follow him that commercials don't need to persuade, inform or even, latterly, charm; all they need to do is dazzle."

Unexpectedly perhaps, Charles Saatchi is equally critical of what he calls the "new cliché of the weird," those beautifully produced minifilms broadcast daily on television with their high production values, strange camera angles, and mystifying slogans. "I keep waiting for old age to take its toll, so I won't be able to tell a decent ad from a bad one," he says. "But I still get worked up about good ads and bad ads, and I see very little that I like at the moment. How can people spend their evenings watching these commercials, and not see that everyone is doing the same thing — it's just weird for the sake of weird."

Nevertheless, his decision to open the doors of the Saatchi Gallery to the likes of Tony Kaye raises many difficult questions. For instance, it is hard to say who has more to lose from such a confrontation of art and commercial art. By exhibiting Foggie Bummer posters that were a campaign for BBC Scotland, screening pop promos for Tanita Tikaram, and putting packaging for

Boots' deodorants on a pedestal, the gallery runs a risk of irreparable damage to its own reputation for seriousness.

Yet even to discuss advertising and art in this way leaves the nagging doubt that it plays the advertising game. The industry has been supremely successful over the last thirty years in refurbishing its public image. Ironically, as the self-important delusions of Charlotte Street were being exposed to some extent by the Saatchi Gallery bonanza, a more immediate challenge to the adman's reputation as a trustworthy professional was arousing concern in some quarters. In May 1995, Adrian Holmes, chairman of advertising agency Lowe Howard Spink, delivered a blistering attack on the decline in moral standards and the rise of what he called "the new unpleasantness, the new brutishness, the new yobbishness" in advertising.

In a keynote speech to the TV95 conference in Monte Carlo, Holmes showed a reel of five TV commercials that had been entered for the British Television Advertising Awards. His main attack was on advertising that offends, uses bad language, degrades people, or promotes aggression. He cited various examples, including an ad for BK sports shoes, by Leagas Shafron Davis Ayer, which showed a lovingly assembled matchstick model being crushed, and an ad for Warr's Harley-Davidson, from Butterfield Day Devito Hockney, in which an elderly man using a walker complained that his son went out and bought a Harley-Davidson for himself instead of using the money to buy his father a wheelchair.

Holmes also criticized a Saatchi & Saatchi campaign for Club 18–30, which was later banned by advertising watchdogs, though not until the day before the posters were due to come down anyway. This campaign greeted the Club 18–30 stereotype of boozy package vacationers in search of "sun, sea, and sex" with billboard slogans like "Beaver España" and "You get two weeks for being drunk and disorderly" and a close-up photograph of a man in boxer shorts next to the copyline "Girls. Can we interest you in a package holiday?" The shocking ads drew widespread media attention, propelling the company's name into the spotlight. To some extent, it was a cynical exercise — according to one Saatchi source, the agency's original brief from the client was to "get banned."

Holmes understands the moral outrage felt by many people who were confronted by the vulgar slogans on street corners and at bus stops. He concedes that advertising does not simply reflect society but shapes it as well. "There is a new desire to shock the audience into taking notice by whatever means," he goes on. "Precisely because they are commercials, in a commercial break, with a logo on the end, all professionally crafted and beautifully lit, they somehow give an official legitimation to what is going on. Commercials don't just sell products; they sell attitudes and behavior with the same targeted efficiency."

The Club 18–30 controversy revived a debate that had focused a couple of months earlier on the billboard campaign advertising Wonderbra. Giant images of scantily clad blonde supermodel Eva Herzigova accompanied by the slogan "Hello boys" provoked hundreds of complaints to the advertising watchdog. Trevor Beattie, creative director of the London-based agency TBWA, which was behind the Wonderbra campaign, takes issue with those who suggest that the ads demeaned women. "Political correctness has caused confusion with the suggestion that you can't have women looking sexy because that makes them passive beings," he insists. "Get real. The Wonderbra campaign was about a woman's right to feel confident about her own sexuality."

Saatchi & Saatchi's defense of its Club 18–30 campaign drew its inspiration from Charles Saatchi's unique vision of advertising twenty-five years earlier. These ads, it was claimed, exactly distilled the values of a Club 18–30 holiday: they would leave no one in any doubt about the kind of holiday they would be buying with this company. They were as simple as the Silk Cut campaign, which used images that illustrated the two words of the brand name to capture the heart of the product. And they were as shocking in their own way as Charles Saatchi's best work for the Health Education Council in the seventies, while being symptomatic of a decade unsure about its moral values or the boundaries of acceptability.

So the new Saatchi agency is launching into a world of advertising and marketing in turmoil. In the spring of 1995 Ed Artzt, chairman and chief executive of Procter & Gamble, told an audience of admen in New York that the company was no longer prepared to hang around in the hope that commercial television would survive on its own. It needed support, he said, and P&G intended to provide it by getting involved in making the programs itself. This was not a new concept for the company. When television first arrived in the U.S. there was no government-owned corporation like the BBC to fill the airwaves with programming, so part of the gap was filled by P&G, which set up its own in-house production department to make programs carrying ads for its products. Even today P&G Productions continues to make three daytime soap operas — so called because they are made by a soap company. Now Artzt was saying that the situation had come full circle and that unless companies like P&G got more involved in program making they would lose any say they had in how programs were paid for. The fear is that television companies might look for new ways to maximize the money they make from programs by having some type of pay-per-view system, making traditional ads redundant. Advertising executives in the U.S. are so afraid of this possibility that they have formed a body called the Coalition for Advertising Supported Information and Entertainment to campaign for the preservation of the commercial break.

In the U.K. there is similar unease, especially as the strength of brand names — advertising's very lifeblood — is being undermined, particularly by the big supermarkets, who are now successfully marketing their own-label products more energetically than ever before. If the eighties celebrated brands and labels as they had never been celebrated before, the nineties has seen the value of even the most famous names of all under attack. Coca-Cola hit back very hard in the so-called Coke Wars last year as entrepreneurs like Richard Branson attempted to steal part of its market with cheaper alternatives.

In the circumstances it is unlikely that Maurice Saatchi will try to remodel his new agency in the image of the old one. According to a former colleague, the younger Saatchi brother is intelligent enough to learn from his mistakes. He adds, "But to really be able to do that requires a certain humility that has not always been shown in the Saatchi temperament. They have a certain tunnel vision. To deny that anything or anyone else really matters can be a huge strength, but it can also be extremely dangerous." Maurice is no exception in being a victim to some extent of his own personality. He still talks about being the biggest and the best, and those who know him well say nothing short of that will satisfy him. Perhaps he would prefer the world not to believe that his unseating has taught him a lesson. In any case, he is not above playing the part.

"The company that Charles and I built has been written up as a vehicle of the eighties," he says. "We founded it in 1970, and it did very well for nearly two decades. Yes, we probably convinced ourselves we could do anything. And yes, I have learned the reason why all those proverbs that have been handed down from our grandmothers like 'Stick to your knitting' have survived. It is because they are true. Presumably, the reason they go on for thousands of years is that people keep on ignoring them."